The Elements of
Figurative Language

The Elements of Composition Series

Series Editor: William A. Covino, Florida Atlantic University

The Elements of Figurative Language

Bradford T. Stull

Rivier College

New York • San Francisco • Boston
London • Toronto • Sydney • Tokyo • Singapore • Madrid
Mexico City • Munich • Paris • Cape Town • Hong Kong • Montreal

Senior Vice President/Publisher: Joseph Opiela
Vice President/Publisher: Eben W. Ludlow
Executive Marketing Manager: Carlise Paulson
Production Manager: Charles Annis
Project Coordination, Text Design, and
  Electronic Page Make-up: Pre-Press Company, Inc.
Cover Designer/Manager: John Callahan
Manufacturing Buyer: Roy Pickering
Printer and Binder: R. R. Donnelly & Sons
Cover Printer: Phoenix Color Corp.

For permission to use copyrighted material, grateful acknowledgment is made
to the copyright holders on page 133, which hereby made part of this copyright page.

Library of Congress Cataloging-in-Publication Data

Stull, Bradford T., 1961–
  The elements of figurative language / Bradford T. Stull.
    p. cm.
  Includes index.
  ISBN 0-205-33712-0 (alk. paper)
    1. Figures of speech. 2. English language—Style. 3. English language—
  Rhetoric. I. Title.

PE1445.A2 S7 2001
808—dc21

2001038609

ISBN 0-205-33712-0

DOH—04 03 02 01

10 9 8 7 6 5 4 3 2 1

This book is for Elias

*As the first-born, he has borne my fatherly
figures the longest, encouraging me always to
move beyond the literal. He is da bomb.*

Contents

2 Figuring Race   25

3 Figuring Class   41

Preface

The tendency of the post-Enlightenment modern world has been to privilege the literal language of science and logic. *The Elements of Figurative Language* doesn't deny the power and importance of literal language, but neither does it denigrate the figurative in favor of the literal. It claims, in fact, that figurative language is central to human life.

The Elements of Figurative Language is intended to help students begin to understand the ways in which humans use figurative language to compose their lifeworlds, to make sense of the human condition. In particular, *The Elements of Figurative Language* focuses on tropes—four tropes especially: metaphor, analogy, irony, and synecdoche.

As postmodern theory and practice has shown, tropes are integral to human life. This book, then, will move students, in a foundational way, into postmodernity. A profound criticism of postmodernity, however, is that it is without an ethic.

The Elements of Figurative Language takes this criticism seriously. After a general introduction to figurative language and tropes in Chapter 1, students will move through a series of "flashpoints" in the ensuing chapters. "Flashpoints" means highly contested, incendiary categories that have been central to the formation of America: race, class, gender, the environment, and war. Students will have the opportunity to examine the ways in which figurative language is central to these dilemmas—central to the ways in which humans have tried to determine the right way of thinking—the right course of action.

As they work their way through these flashpoints, students will encounter a range of texts from many genres. Figurative language is not the property of poetry alone, but is part of expositions, speeches, letters, and the like. Each chapter includes both analytic and constructive exercises. The analytic exercises ask students to analyze a text or set of texts. The constructive exercises ask students to compose original work, to build new language worlds.

The Elements of Figurative Language is appropriate for a range of readers, from first-year students in composition courses learning to analyze and construct figures to early graduate students beginning to work deeply with and in rhetoric theory.

Acknowledgments

If books are the extension of an author's energy, they are also then filled with the energy of people who, in their own ways, inform the author. These folk need to be acknowledged, lights all. First, William A. Covino and Eben W. Ludlow, professor and publisher, gentlemen each. They encouraged me to pursue this book, allowing me to explore some of my deepest concerns. Second, Mrs. Leatha Warenda and Mrs. Barbara Carpenter, great teachers both. I began to write this book as my son emerged from their kindergarten, and I saw in them the possibilities of teaching at its best. Third, my family, true delights. They provide me with energy—limitless and nearly unimaginable.

The Elements of
Figurative Language

1

Figuring

A Vignette

Language is a communicative device, without doubt. It is used to question, to demand, to plead, to whine, to moan, to praise, to love, to hate. In short, it allows humans—and perhaps other creatures—to express themselves, to make themselves known. Imagine, for instance, that you are twelve years old. Once again you—or most likely your mother—has misplaced your favorite sneakers. Those gems that—as Ray Bradbury says of the sneakers just purchased by the lead character in *Dandelion Wine*—allow you to jump higher, run faster, are missing.

> You ask, with just a hint of irritation in your voice,
> "Mom, where are my Nikes?"
> "I don't know, honey."
> Absorbed reading *Harry Potter and the Goblet of Fire* for the fifth time, you turn to your younger brother.
> "Dork. Find my Nikes for me."
> "Find them yourself."
> You turn again to mom.
> "Mom? Could you please find my Nikes? I have to finish reading about Mad Eye Moody."
> "Sweetpea, I am too busy making your lunches. Check the porch."

Ignoring the way in which your mother has said "I am too busy"—did you really notice a hint of annoyance?—you speak to no one in particular, but to everyone within hearing.

"I might as well be living by myself in the Arctic for all the help people give me around here."

Your father sticks his head into your room.

"That can be arranged, darlin'. Flights leave twice daily."

You put the book down and do, indeed, find the Nikes, but not on the porch. They never made it that far. They were left outside. In the rain.

"Crap. Crap, crap, crap."

Your little brother hears you.

"I'm telling Mom."

You both charge in.

"Mom, she said crap."

"Mom, my Nikes are shelled."

Your mother ignores your little brother, for the time being.

"Why did you leave them out?"

You look crestfallen.

"Mom, I have to have these today. I just have to."

Your mother stops the inquisition.

"We can dry them, but next time use the head God gave you."

Fifteen minutes later, the Nikes are ready to go.

"Thanks, Mom. You're a gem."

You think to yourself, "I love these babies."

You say to your younger brother, whom you haven't forgiven for telling your mother that you said "crap,"

"Thanks to you too, twerp."

He says, running,

"I am rubber, you are glue. Whatever you say bounces off me and sticks to you."

This vignette indicates how language, in manifold ways, allows us to move through our lives, to express our needs, our wants, and our desires, even as they are in confluence with, and compete against, the needs, the wants, and the desires of others. Yet, it also shows that while language is a communicative device, it is not only that. It also expresses and shapes worldviews through the combination of literal and figurative language. We will return to a discussion of this vignette later in the chapter. For now, we need to consider three important terms: worldview, literal language, and figurative language.

Literal Language, Figurative Language, and Worldviews

Not surprisingly, the term "worldview" refers to ways in which people view the world. The phrase "view the world," however, is not quite as easy to understand as it might first appear. The word "view" is not used literally. Primarily it is a metaphor. Although one's worldview might include what one has gained from viewing, with one's eyes, the world around, it is more that that. It includes, certainly, the other senses: what one hears, what one feels, what one tastes, and what one smells. It also includes feelings, desires, thoughts, ruminations, revelations, and memories. It includes, in short, one's outlook on the world as this outlook arises from the entirety of one's person.

Likewise, the word "world" is not a simple term. It is, finally, metonymic. "Metonymic" means to take manifold phenomena and reduce/condense/crystallize them into one point. The word "worldview" takes those very sensations, feelings, desires, thoughts, ruminations, revelations, memories, and the like that constitute both who we are and how we view the world around us. "World," as slippery as it is, is something that we can hold in front of us, manipulate, objectify, and view.

Worldviews, broadly conceived, are expressed either in literal or figurative language. On the whole, literal language is that language favored by scientists, logicians, mathematicians, and the like. The definition of literal language, like that of figurative, can be approached negatively or positively. Positively, literal language is that language that seeks to speak plainly, to speak directly about that subject under examination. Negatively, literal language is not figurative: it is language that avoids the use of devices like metaphor, analogy, synecdoche, and irony. Of course, the problem with negative definitions is that the terms are always wholly dependent on what they are not. If you don't understand what they are not, it is difficult to understand, clearly, what they are. What is literal language? Language that is not figurative. What, then, is figurative language?

Figurative language is the language, on the whole, favored by rhetoricians, poets, fiction writers, lovers, and the like. Negatively, figurative language is the language that avoids speaking directly or plainly about the subject under examination. Positively, figurative language is the language that either speaks symbolically about the subject or heightens the musicality of the language when speaking about the subject. This book concentrates entirely on the first meaning of figurative language: the act of speaking in "language symbols."

This book is concerned about figurative language in general and four main types in particular: metaphor, analogy, synecdoche, and irony. Although these terms will be treated at length later in the chapter, keep these definitions in mind:

- **Metaphor:** To claim that something is what it literally is not
- **Analogy:** To construct a comparative relationship between four terms
- **Synecdoche:** To discuss a part as it represents the whole, or vice versa
- **Irony:** To discover or construct the opposite of the apparent meaning

The careful reader will remember that only a few sentences ago I claimed that figurative language is said to be "the language that speaks symbolically." The term "symbolically" is then unpacked to mean "language symbols": "the act of speaking in language symbols."

This move has been made for two reasons. First, I wanted to accommodate the musical demands of the first sentence. The sentence required a parallel verb structure: speaks and heightens. To have introduced at that point "speaking in language symbols" would have disrupted the parallel music: the sentence would have grated. Yet, I also knew that the phrase "to speak symbolically" was problematic. Formal logicians and mathematicians would argue that their language is highly symbolic (hence the discipline, symbolic logic), but I am not sure that they would want to say that their languages are figurative. By "language symbols" I mean language that is explicitly not literal: language refigured in order to elucidate, illuminate, hint, provoke, and prod, but not to speak plainly.

Two examples will make the characteristics of, and differences between, literal and figurative language clear. The scene? A candlelit dinner for two at a cozy café near Lincoln Park, in Chicago. The characters? Two lovers.

> Take One:
> Marion turns to Michael, gazes deeply into his eyes, says, "I see moonlit pools."
> Take Two:
> Marion turns to Michael, gazes deeply into his eyes, says, "I see two blue irises."
> Take Three:
> Marion turns to Michael, gazes deeply into his eyes, says, "I see two round contractile membranes, each with blue pigment."

In Take One, Marion is speaking figuratively, or more precisely, metaphorically. At this moment of passion and romance, at this moment when she wants to express her love for Michael, she turns, as humans often do, not to the literal language of science, or logic of mathematics, but to the figurative, metaphorical language of rhetoric and poetry. She sees his eyes, but more than his eyes. She sees, indeed, two moonlit pools. Does she literally see pools? No. Or, not unless she and Michael live in a world where, literally, human eyes are moonlit pools. The refiguring of Michael's eyes into moonlit pools helps Marion to express her worldview both to herself and Michael. His eyes are more than organic tissue: they are a place of romance, mystery, love, and this is the world in which she places herself, which she expresses, which she names.

In Take Two, Marion begins to shift out of this figurative world into a literal one. Rather than moonlit pools, she sees in Michael's eyes two blue irises. This, of course, might chill the romance of the evening. She is shifting not only language, but worldview: no longer is she lover, or, more fairly, lover only. No longer is Michael the beloved. Marion has become a field researcher, looking into her subject's eyes. In these eyes, she finds not the mystery of passion, of romance, of desire, but, rather, physical objects that she describes plainly. Explicitly she names the color: blue. The blue marks not pools, but irises.

Strangely, however, the word "irises" still could be read figuratively. "Iris," after all, scientifically names that part of the eye that immediately surrounds the pupil. It is the part that holds color. When we say that a person's "eyes" are blue, we really mean that the irises are blue. Yet, "iris" also names a flower, and a sensual one at that. It has curving petals that both reveal and conceal the center, the place that bees, in their desirous, passionate flights, seek. Has then Marion shifted into literal language, or has she simply shifted figures? Is the field researcher plainly describing the physical characteristics of her observed subject, or is she the lover once again, layering another metaphor of romance on her besotted beloved?

The ambiguity of the word "iris" reveals the power in Kenneth Burke's assertion that to study words like "iris" in this context is "an evanescent moment" where "the dividing line between the figurative and the literal usages shift" (*Grammar of Motives* 1969, p. 503). What he means is this: a word like iris—as it is found in this context—is vaporous. It seems to have substance, but when we try to grab it, we can't. We close our hands around the vapor, and the vapor flows through our fingers. So, when we study the word "iris" as Marion's literal attempt to describe what she sees, the "literal" becomes "figurative": the iris as plainly part of the eye becomes floral, a metaphor.

Take Three shifts Marion cleanly into the role of field observer, or, perhaps, laboratory clinician. Gone are the moonlit pools. Gone are the irises with their double meaning. Instead, she moves into another realm, a realm of plain, literal, clinical language: "I see two round contractile membranes, each with blue pigment." Michael, unless he is not listening, is in no doubt about Marion's worldview and his place in it. He is not the beloved at this moment, but a subject of study. His response? It depends on his own worldview. Does he want to be the beloved? The clinical subject? Both?

Back to the Vignette

With this discussion of worldview and literal and figurative language in mind, we return to the vignette about the lost Nikes, this time with enumerated sections so that we can look at them more carefully.

1. You ask, with just a hint of irritation in your voice, "Mom, where are my Nikes?"

2. "I don't know, honey."

3. Absorbed reading *Harry Potter and the Goblet of Fire* for the fifth time, you turn to your younger brother.

4. "Dork. Find my Nikes for me."

5. "Find them yourself."

6. You turn again to mom. "Mom? Could you please find my Nikes? I have to finish reading about Mad Eye Moody."

7. "Sweetpea, I am too busy making your lunches. Check the porch."

8. Ignoring the way in which your mother has said "I am too busy making"—did you really notice a hint of annoyance?—you speak to no one in particular, but to everyone within hearing. "I might as well be living by myself in the Arctic for all the help people give me around here."

9. Your father sticks his head into your room. "That can be arranged, darlin'. Flights leave twice daily."

10. You put the book down and do, indeed, find the Nikes, but not on the porch. They never made it that far. They were left outside. In the rain. "Crap. Crap, crap, crap."

11. Your little brother hears you. "I'm telling Mom."

12. You both charge in. "Mom, she said crap." "Mom, my Nikes are shelled."

13. Your mother ignores your little brother, for the time being. "Why did you leave them out?"

14. You look crestfallen. "Mom, I have to have these today. I just have to."

15. Your mother stops the inquisition. "We can dry them, but next time use the head God gave you."

16. Fifteen minutes later, the Nikes are ready to go. "Thanks, Mom. You're a gem."

17. You think to yourself, "I love these babies."

18. You say to your younger brother, whom you haven't forgiven for telling your mother that you said "crap," "Thanks to you too, twerp."

19. He says, running, "I am rubber, you are glue. Whatever you say bounces off me and sticks to you."

We see in this vignette a play of literal and figurative language, all of which expresses these family members' worldviews. Line 1, for instance, is telling because it uses a metaphor that most don't recognize. The daughter asks her mother about her Nikes, which all North Americans know to be sneakers marked by the infamous "swoosh." In the world of sneaker manufacturing and marketing, literally, the word Nike indicates a company whose headquarters are in Eugene, Oregon, a company that has come to dominate the athletic shoe landscape. The fact that the daughter has Nike shoes indicates that part of her worldview is that shared by many in North America: these shoes are valuable, prized possessions, more important than other sneakers, even though other sneakers might perform just as well.

Metaphorically, Nike refers to the Greek goddess of victory. Presumably, when the company we now literally call "Nike" claimed this mythological name for itself, it wanted a symbol: it wanted people to join a worldview in which wearing a pair of Nike sneakers allows the wearer to participate, at least figuratively, in the world of the goddess. It is not dissimilar to Christians wearing crosses in order to make and mark a worldview in which Jesus Christ has an important place. Nor is it dissimilar to Jews who wear a Star of David to make and mark a worldview in which the Abrahamic covenant between YHWH and the people of God has an important place. The company and the shoes are not literally the goddess of victory (if we can even suggest that a mythological figure can be literal). Rather, the company is refiguring language in order to make a symbolic claim. Whether or not the wearer, this daughter, is consciously aware that she bears, and thus participates in the world of Greek goddesses, does not matter. She does: the metaphor demands it.

The mother's use of terms of endearment like "honey" in line 2 and "sweetpea" in line 7 demonstrates her own participation in a figurative world and thus indicates parts of her own worldview. Obviously, the daughter is neither honey nor a sweetpea, literally, plainly, empirically. She is a female human. Yet, the mother refigures language in order to mark a relationship with her daughter. She is sweet, like honey. She is beautiful and delicate, like a sweetpea flower. No doubt, the mother has probably felt this way about her daughter since her daughter emerged from the womb. The daughter is other than a female human born of the mother. She is a delight, part of a mother's worldview in which her children are special, lovely, delicious.

That the mother calls the daughter "honey" in line 2 is also worthy of attention because she does so having heard that the daughter has spoken with irritation in line 1. The tone is accusatory, even though she is asking a question. The mother, saint that she is, ignores the daughter's presumption—that the mother should and does know where the shoes are and is, probably, hiding them deliberately. With a term of endearment, she responds simply, "I don't know." This hints at an ironic edge that runs through the vignette. With a tone of irritation, the daughter, the beloved honey and sweetpea, is beginning to talk to her mother like a demanding, spoiled princess. The irony, to be sure, is that the sweet flower is perhaps not so sweet after all.

The vignette's ironic elements emerge fully in line 18, when the daughter "thanks" her brother. This "thanks," we know, is hardly sincere, hardly literal. It is, in fact, highly ironic or, more precisely, highly sarcastic: she means the opposite of what she has said, and she means it meanly. Literally, what she means is something like this: "I don't appreciate the fact that you told mom that I said the word 'crap.'" The worldview both revealed by and supported by this ironic use of "thanks" includes a view of her brother as someone not worth treating well, with kindness: he is nearly beneath contempt.

As unbelievable as it may seem, this discussion could continue on for many, many more pages. Figurative language is complex and worthy of intense study because it reveals worldviews. Or, as Kenneth Burkes suggests in his study of metaphor, metonymy, synecdoche, and irony, they help discover and describe "'the truth'" (*The Grammar of Motives* 1969, p. 503). To be sure, this truth is perhaps different than the truth discovered by the literal language of scientists, logicians, and mathematicians.

It is, nonetheless, truth, albeit a truth with a lowercase "t," albeit truth in quotation marks. The worldviews that are expressed in, supported by, challenged through figurative words are no less "true" than the truth that $1 + 1 = 2$, if by truth one means that which is actual or that which exists. Granted, the literal language of $1 + 1 = 2$ is more stable than the ironic use of the word "thanks" by the daughter in the vignette. Nonetheless, the word "thanks," spoken sarcastically, reveals what exists, what is actual, in the daughter's worldview: her brother is a bother.

Hinted at here is this: the literal languages of science, of logic, of mathematics, important and beautiful as they are, are not the only ways to express, support, challenge, and change human worldviews. As is well-known, we live in an age when the literal languages of science, of logic, of mathematics, are highly prized, seen as the ways in which humans can construct better worlds and thus better worldviews. This book offers a challenge to this: the world of figurative language can complement the world of literal language. We can, in the terms of Aristotle, be rounded: we can embrace not only the literal, but the figurative, not only logic, but rhetoric and poetics as well.

Four Tropes: Metaphor, Analogy, Synecdoche, Irony

The term "figurative language" itself is a figure: it is a reduction/condensation/crystallization (metonymy) for a vast field of language strategies. As I suggested previously, what is not part of the this book's discussion are those "figures" that attend to the musicality of language. It does not attend to figures like "anadiplosis," which Edward P.J. Corbett and Robert J. Connors define as the "repetition of the last word of one clause at the beginning of the following clause" (*Style and Statement* 1999, p. 56). An example of "anadiplosis" is the following: "I love green fields, fields love gentle rain, rain loves the sky under which I lay."

The importance and power of this dimension of figurative language is not to be dismissed. Indeed, speakers such as Martin Luther King, Jr., make great use of figurative language in this way. What else is the great dream sequence in "I Have a Dream" than "anaphora," that figure that names the "repetition of the same word or group of words at the beginning of successive clauses" (Corbett and Connor 54)?

That said, this book focuses on the other dimension of figurative language: what I called "language symbols" earlier, but what are more appropriately called "tropes." In particular, this book focuses on four tropes: metaphor, analogy, synecdoche, and irony. Although these are discussed in greater detail later in this chapter, it is important to establish at this point what, exactly, "trope" means. The problem with this previous sentence, however, lays in the phrase "what, exactly, 'trope' means." The problem is this: the word "trope" is itself a metaphor. From the Greek *tropos*, to conceive and deploy a "trope" is "to turn" the word, the concept. It goes without saying that one does not literally turn a word when one conceives and deploys, for instance, a metaphor. Consider, again, the vignette with which this chapter began. When the daughter anguishes, in line 12, that her Nikes are "shelled," she means that they are ruined. ("Ruined" itself has metaphorical implications: the shoes have become ruins, remnants of the glorious construction that they once were.) Metaphorically, the shoes no longer have substance: they are merely shells of what once they were. The daughter has not literally turned anything. Rather, she sees her shoes and conceives them symbolically, as a trope, a metaphor.

Flashpoints

Thus far, in all its discussion, this book has dwelt on rather familiar examples: family life and love. This is not to say that family life is unimportant, that love is ordinary, as the word "familiar" suggests. Rather, these examples were chosen in order to make a point: figurative language, specifically tropes, are a part of the weave of all parts of our lives, even those we walk most often. They are not simply the provence of poets, of novelists, of dramatists, of orators, or of professional wordsmiths. They inhabit all aspects of human beings, giving shape to, and being shaped by, our worldviews.

The remainder of this book, however, turns from these more familiar areas to what can be called "flashpoints." "Flashpoint," scientifically, literally, refers to the "lowest temperature at which the vapor of a combustible liquid can be made to ignite momentarily" (*American Heritage College Dictionary*). Metaphorically, it suggests a moment of incendiary reaction, violence, conflict, and challenge. The book turns from the familiar to the flashpoint not to belittle the familiar but to explore the ways in which metaphor, analogy, synecdoche, and irony inform, and are informed by, these flashpoints, all of which are of central importance to human beings at this point in our history.

The flashpoints around which this book revolves are five areas of pressing human concern: race, class, gender, the natural environment, and war. Three—race, class, gender—have dominated recent discussions of American culture. The other two—the environment and war—are of growing concern. We all live in a time of ecological danger, a time marked by global warfare and warfare around the globe.

Genres: Expository Essay, Speech, Poem, Letter

Although the previous discussion of flashpoints may indicate otherwise, this book is not about political science or sociology. It is, rather, a book about figurative language. In order to study the way in which language figures human life, the book studies how four types of tropes in particular "turn" around/in/about/on certain flashpoints. In order to study this figuring, this book must turn to examples: actual language in use.

Though poetry is considered, this is not simply a book about the ways in which *poets* involved with flashpoints conceive and deploy tropes. Though speeches are considered, neither is this book simply about the ways in which *orators* involved with flashpoints conceive and deploy tropes. Though essays are considered, this book is not simply about the ways in which *essayists* involved with flashpoints conceive and deploy tropes. Though the pastoral letter is considered, this is not simply a book about the ways in which *letter writers* involved with flashpoints conceive and deploy tropes. The book considers all these genres, recognizing that public conversation takes many. We would do well to be able to read all these genres effectively, and to write them as well.

Genre, as a term, is a categorical word. It indicates a set, or class, of compositional practice. In poetry, for instance, one might look for, or write with, stanzas, intentional line breaks, rhyme, and meter. In letters, one might look for, or write with, personal address, familiar language. In speeches, one might look for, or write with, the repetition of phrases, the use of crescendo. In essays, one might look for, or write with, a "thesis" with supporting points and subpoints.

Genres, it must be said, do blend together: there is no hard and fast line between them. There can be, and is, for example, "prose poetry." This blended genre places together features of prose (like running lines from left to write without intentional line breaks) and poetry (like heightened attention to rhythm, meter, and sound). However, even in this hybrid, "prose" is the adjective and "poetry" the noun. The best prose poems are distinctly not prose in the way an editorial in a local newspaper is prose.

So too poetry and oration often blend. For example, consider these lines from Shakespeare's *Hamlet*, spoken by the King in Act IV, Scene 7:

He made a confession of you;
And gave you such a masterly report,
For art and exercise in your defense,
And for your rapier most especially,
That he cried out, 'twould be a sight indeed,
If one could match you: The scrimers of their nation,
He swore, had neither motion, guard, nor eye,
If you oppos'd them. Sir, this report of his
Did Hamlet so envenom with his envy
That he could nothing do but wish and beg
Your sudden coming o'er to play with him.

Is this a poem or a speech? Both. Its poetic dimensions are evident, for instance, in its line breaks. It uses "enjambment" throughout, meaning that it breaks the lines so that the grammar of the sentences are broken as well. So, the last two lines read, in part, "wish and beg / Your sudden coming." Had the next-to-the-last line ended with grammatical ending of the sentence, "Your sudden coming . . ." would have to be moved up. Such a choice, however, would have broken the relatively consistent length of the lines throughout the poem. Prose, or a speech, would have not attended to line breaks in this way. The speech would simply be written out left to write, across the full width of the page, just as these sentences that you are now reading do not attend to line breaks. The lines break only because the page width breaks them.

The King's poem, however, is also an oration. The King and Laertes are discussing Hamlet in this particular scene. Laertes mostly prods the King with questions and statements, and the King responds at length. Formally, this is part of a dramatic dialogue, but its placement in the play also shows how genres blur: is it poetry? is it oration? is it drama? The King takes the opportunity to deliver a series of short orations in order to convince Laertes of a certain action: to kill Hamlet under the subterfuge of fencing practice. The King wants Laertes to revenge his father's murder by murdering Hamlet in turn. As the King says, "you may choose / A sword unbated, and in a pass of practice / Requite him for your father."

This book, then, asks you to put aside the modern reluctance to consider multiple genres at the same time. Typically, one takes a poetry class to read and write poetry. One takes a speech communication class to read and write speeches. One takes a composition class to read and write essays. The letter? It is read only as part of larger classes (say, early American literature) and almost never taught as a genre in which one can write.

Postmodernity

In asking you to put aside the modern reluctance to consider multiple genres at the same time, this book asks you to move into another world, what can be called the "postmodern world." No genre is given primary place in this text, considered more valuable or worthy than any other. Nor is the act of reading—analysis—given primary place over the act of composition—building. Typically, schools educate readers: we learn to read poetry, drama, essays, letters, speeches, advertisements, and the like. Only in special cases are students asked to compose: in the first year composition classroom, in special classes devoted to "creative writing" or public speaking. This book asks its readers to think of themselves as both readers and composers, analysts and builders. Throughout, each exercise includes both analytic and constructive tasks in the four genres under consideration: you will enter into the postmodern blend of genres, of tasks.

Further, these texts will demand that you enter into, and consider seriously, multiple and conflicting worldviews, worldviews that you might find dangerous, comforting, challenging. You will be asked to consider, in Chapters 2–6,

- W.E.B. Du Bois' intellectual Black activist refiguring made manifest in his editorials written for *The Crisis*.
- The American Roman Catholic Bishops' theopolitical refiguring, written into their pastoral letter on the economy.
- Sojourner Truth's religious feminist refiguring, as recorded in a speech.
- Gary Snyder's Native American/Buddhist refiguring, seen in his poetry.
- Abraham Lincoln's civic Protestant refiguring, as found in his "Second Inaugural Address."

Before we turn to these chapters, we turn now to a more detailed consideration of the tropes under consideration: metaphor, analogy, synecdoche, and irony.

Metaphor

Metaphor is probably the most discussed of the four tropes at play in this book. The earliest explicit discussions of the nature and characteristics of metaphor quite possibly appear in Aristotle's works, particularly *On Rhetoric* and *Poetics*. In *Poetics* (21.7), Aristotle defines metaphor as "a movement of an alien name either from genus to species or from species to genus or by analogy" (Artistotle, *On Rhetoric*, ed. George Kennedy 222 n.25). College students are quite likely to remember this definition of metaphor given to them by their high school teachers: the comparison of two things without using the words "like" or "as." Metaphor's partner, "simile," then, is the comparison of two things using like or as.

Kenneth Burke, for his part, suggests that we think about metaphor as "a device for seeing something *in terms* of something else" (*Grammar of Motives* 1969, p. 503). This is to say, we will say that "x" is "y" in order to understand "x" in a way that we have not yet understood it. Differing from simile, metaphor suggests that symbolically there is complete identification between "x" and "y." For instance, one lover might say to another, "your lips are roses." Are the lips literally roses? Of course not. Symbolically, are they? Absolutely. X is y in this case: the lips are roses in this symbolic action. The worldview of the lover includes nature, especially that of flowers. When the lover sees the beloved, indeed kisses the beloved, the lover sees not a world of computers, a world of concrete, of sports, but of the natural, flowering order of existence.

Just as the two basic parts of English are nouns and verbs, so, too, metaphors can be either nouns or verbs. An example of a noun metaphor is as follows: "That test was a bear." Was the test literally a bear? No. Metaphorically, however, it was: it was difficult, big, mean, grumpy, what-have-you. "Bear," a noun in the position of the direct object of this sentence, suggests, again, a world of nature, beyond urban or suburban order. The following sentence reveals a verb metaphor: "Ameeka flew to the grocery store near her house." Did she, literally? Of course not. Did she, metaphorically? Absolutely. Ameeka's action was such that the observer needed to use this metaphor to describe her actions with some kind of justice. The worldview revealed here is the fantastic, an imagined place where humans can fly without aid of an airplane.

❖ *Exercise 1.1*

What follows are three sentences, drawn from various texts. Each includes at least one metaphor. Analyze these sentences. Locate and name the metaphor(s), and state whether they are nouns or verbs. Then, name and discuss the worldview(s) from which the metaphor emerges, which the metaphor supports.

1. They had only their hard fists to batter at the world with (Willa Cather, *My Antonia* 1977, p. 55).

2. If violence can be justified at all, its terror must have the tempo of a surgeon's skill and healing must follow quickly upon its wounds (Reinhold Niebuhr, *Moral Man and Immoral Society* 1960, p. 220).

3. University teachers are supposed to be men [sic] with special knowledge and special training such as should fit them to approach controversial questions in a manner peculiarly likely to throw light upon them (Bertrand Russell, "Freedom and the Colleges" in *Why I Am Not a Christian* 1957, p. 180).

❖ *Exercise 1.2*

Exercise 1.1 asked you to think analytically: You looked at the work of others and, like chemists in lab, removed parts of the whole solution in order to understand both the parts and the whole. What follows are two brief constructive exercises. Rather than analyzing the metaphors of others, you will construct your own.

1. Compose a question concerning one of the flashpoints central to this book. The question should not be answerable with either a "yes" or a "no." Then, compose a one sentence answer to the question, using a noun metaphor in the sentence. Finally, discuss the nature of the metaphor,

concentrating especially on the worldview from which it emerges, which it supports.

2. Compose a question concerning one of the flashpoints central to this book. The question should not be answerable with either a "yes" or a "no." Then, compose a one sentence answer to the question, using a verb metaphor in the sentence. Finally, discuss the nature of the metaphor, concentrating especially on the worldview from which it emerges, which it supports.

Analogy

Aristotle, framing much of the subsequent conversation about analogy, wants to name it as a subcategory of metaphor (*Rhetoric* 3.7 and also in *Poetics* 21). It is true that some analogies are explicitly metaphorical. Indeed, at some point all the tropes imply the others. That said, analogies do have distinct features, as a reading of Aristotle's *Poetics* reveals. There he lays out a definition that informs such contemporary standard examinations as the SAT, the ACT, and the Miller Analogy Test (MAT).

In the *Poetics*, Aristotle writes that

> I call it analogy when the second thing is related to the first as the fourth is to the third; for [a poet] will say the fourth for the second or the second for the fourth. 12. And sometimes they add something to which it relates in place of what it [usually] refers to. I mean, for example, the cup is related to Dionysus as the shield to Ares. [The poet] will then say that the cup is the shield of Dionysus and the shield the cup of Ares. (Cited in *On Rhetoric*, trans. George Kennedy 296).

Familiar to Aristotle's readers, but perhaps not so familiar to the contemporary American audience, are the identities of Dionysus and Ares. Both are members of the Olympic pantheon, Gods granted thrones on Olympus by Zeus himself. Ares is also known by his Roman name, Mars. He is the God of war and as such carries a shield. Dionysus, in contrast, is the God of wine, of merriment. As such, he carries a cup, a cup of wine to be exact.

For Aristotle, analogy figures relationships like all tropes, but in a particular way: it uses two sets of two terms at their most basic level. The first set has an internal relationship that is matched by the second set.

This also allows for a movement between terms in each of the sets. Consider this:

A = cup

B = Dionysus

C = shield

D = Ares

As Aristotle states it, A is to B as C is to D. Given this, the clever poet will claim that A is the C of B: The cup is the shield of Dionysus. This, of course, is what makes Aristotle say that analogy is a form of metaphor. To say that the cup is the shield of Dionysus is to take the terms of an analogy and give the metaphorical properties: the cup is no longer a cup, but a shield.

Nonetheless, the analogy in its original form is not necessarily a metaphor. Rather, it is a figure of language that expresses a set of like relationships among two sets of terms. In essence, the analogy does not claim total identification, which is the property of the metaphor. It claims a similarity of relationships.

The expression of the relationships may be either implicit or explicit, which is Aristotle's point when he says that

> In some cases there is no corresponding term within the analogy, but none the less a likeness will be expressed; for example, scattering seed is sowing, but in the case of the sun the [disperson of light] has no name [in Greek]. Nevertheless, this has the same relation to the sun as scattering has to seed, so it is expressed as "sowing divine fire." The phrase "sowing divine fire" is certainly metaphorical: the sun becomes "divine fire" and the act of dispersion of the sun's rays becomes "sowing."

The phrase at its root, however, is an analogy:

A=sowing

B=seed

C=the dispersion of light

D=sun

Thus, sowing is to seed as the dispersion of light is to the sun. The phrase "sowing divine fire" is an implied analogy: the analogy is not stated explicitly but rather implicitly. To say it explicitly would, as good writers know, be tantamount to a crime: the music of language would be lost in the careful attention to explicit language. Analogies, however, are often explicit, as you will see in the following exercises.

❖ Exercise 1.3

What follows is a section from Catherine MacKinnon's book, *Only Words* (1993), in which she argues against pornography. Analyze this selection. Locate and name the analogies. Then, name and discuss the worldview(s) from which the analogies emerge, which the analogies support. Because MacKinnon's use of analogy is very subtle, key analogical terms are marked by me. Keep in mind that she is comparing two types of "consumers" and actions that they might, or might not, take.

> ... There is no evidence that *consumers of racist propaganda* aggress against *the target of the literature* whether or not they agree with the positions it takes. This is not to say that such material works wholly on the conscious level, but rather that it does not primarily work by circumventing conscious processes. The same can be said for nonsexually explicit misogynist literature. With *pornography*, by contrast, *consumers* see women as less than human, and even rape them, without being aware that an "idea" promoting that content, far less a political position in favor of the sexualized inequality of the sexes, is being advanced. (p. 62)

❖ Exercise 1.4

Exercise 1.3 asked you to think analytically: You looked at Catherine MacKinnon's work and, like chemists in lab, removed parts of the whole solution in order to understand both the parts and the whole. MacKinnon herself names and advances her analogy. She says, just a few sentences later, that "nothing analogous to the sexual response has been located as the mechanism of racism, or as the mechanism of response to sexist material that is not sexual" (62). She claims that her fundamental analogy, with which she compares consumers of racist propaganda to consumers of pornography, is negative. It seems similar, but is not. Consumers of pornography, she argues, act out the pornography by violating women's bodies. Consumers of racist propaganda, in contrast, do not.

The constructive task:

Choose one of the flashpoints about which this book is concerned. Construct a question that cannot be answered with either "yes" or "no." Answer this question in a passage of two paragraphs. Place at least one analogy at the center of your answer: use the two paragraphs to develop it.

Synecdoche

"Synecdoche" is, by far, the strangest of these four tropes: it is the one with which students are most unfamiliar in terms of the word itself. Conceptually, as it will become clear, synecdoche has the same place that all the tropes have: it is omnipresent. As a word, however, it is rarely used in polite company.

Kenneth Burke, in his own work with the term synecdoche, offers this:

> If I reduce the contours of the United States, for instance, to the terms of a relief map, I have within these limits "represented" the United States. As a mental state is the "representation" of certain material conditions, so we could—reversing the process—say that material conditions are "representative" of the mental state. That is, if there is some kind of correspondence between what we call the act of perception and what we call the thing perceived, then either of these equivalents can be taken as "representative" of the other. (*Grammar of Motives*, p. 507)

Central to Burke's discussion of synecdoche is this: the word "representation." It appears three times, suggesting then that central to synecdoche is the act of representation. The relief map of the United States, for example, represents the United States. Is it the United States literally? No. Is it synecdochally? Yes. The map is not metaphorical because the map does not claim that the United States is something that it literally is not: Canada, for example. Instead, the relief map portrays the geography of United States as it is, but in representative form.

As Burke writes, synecdoche is "the part for the whole, whole for the part, container for the contained, sign for the thing signified, material for the thing made, cause for effect, effect for cause, genus for species, species for genus, etc." (*Grammar of Motives,* pp. 507–8). A prime example of this in political terms is the Congress of the United States of America. Divided into two bodies, the House of Representatives and the Senate, the Congress is fundamentally synecdochal. Each member of the House represents a whole of which she or he is a part: the Congressional District in his or her home state. Theoretically, each member of the House is elected to represent the people who live and work in that District: each member of the House sits in the House not for himself or herself but for the larger body of which she or he is a part. The Congressional Districts themselves are understood to be parts of a whole: each stands not as an island unto itself but as a part of the State in which it resides. Of course, the synecdochal play continues: each state is not an island, but a representative part of a larger whole, which is the country called the United States of America.

So, too, Senators are synecdochal figures. Each state is allowed two Senators. Each Senator, theoretically, represents not portions of each state, but the entire state that has elected them. The Honorable Senators from New Hampshire, for instance, sit in the Senate only because they have been elected to represent the people who live in New Hampshire. They are not there to pursue their own personal interests, but the interests of the state itself. When they vote, they vote the state, at least synecdochally. The "state," of course, is also synecdochal. It is a term we use, and a governmental body we empower, to represent us, the people.

Consider, finally, the term "governmental body," which is frequently part of the discussions surrounding "representative" government. As a metaphor, it points to the worldview implied in any form of representative democracy: that of the integral relationships of the organic form we know as the body. The president of the United States, for instance, is often referred to as the "head" of state. The "right" and the "left" of the major political parties are often referred to as wings. Ronald Reagan, for instance, was considered to be part of the "right wing" of the Republican Party. Any member of Congress is considered to be the "voice" of the people that she or he represents. The worldview, then, of a representative democracy is that of the body: we all are part of an organic whole.

❖ Exercise 1.5

What follows is a section of St. Paul's "Letter to the Corinthians" (12:14–21), in which he attempts to shore up the nascent community of believers in Corinth. Locate and name the synecdoche (ies). Then, name and discuss the worldview(s) from which the synecdoches emerge, which the synecdoches supports. You will notice, undoubtedly, other tropes as well.

> Nor is the body to be identified with any one of its many parts. If the foot were to say, "I am not the hand and so I do not belong to the body," would not that mean that it stopped being part of the body? If the ear were to say, "I am not an eye, and so I do not belong to the body," would that mean it is not a part of the body? If your whole body was just one eye, how would you hear anything? If it was just one ear, how would you smell anything?
>
> Instead of that, God put all the separate parts into the body on purpose. If all the parts were the same, how could it be a body? As it is, the parts are many but the body is one. The eye cannot say to the hand, "I do not need you," nor can the head say to the feet, "I do not need you."

❖ Exercise 1.6

Exercise 1.5 asked you to think analytically, to study the work of St. Paul in order to discuss the ways in which he uses synecdoche and the worldview that the synecdoche supports. This exercise is a constructive task.

Choose one of the flashpoints about which this book is concerned. Compose a question that cannot be answered with either "yes" or "no." Answer this question in a passage of two paragraphs. Place at least one synecdoche at the center of your answer: use the two paragraphs to develop it.

Irony

Irony, like all the tropes, is an omnipresent part of human life. Its most obvious form is sarcasm. Return briefly to the earlier discussion of irony and sarcasm near the beginning of this chapter.

The vignette about the daughter searching for her misplaced Nikes has at least one ironic, in particular, sarcastic, moment: when the daughter "thanks" her brother. The "thanks" is really no thanks at all. She has used one word to say what she wants to say, but what she wants to say is really the opposite of what she said. In a phrase, then, irony is present when the word, the event, the situation actually demonstrates the opposite of its apparent meaning.

With irony, opposites are never excluded (Kenneth Burke, *Grammar of Motives*, p. 512). Indeed, the opposites work together to reveal the meaning. This is most clearly seen when Burke refers to Marxist thought about history in *Grammar of Motives*. He quotes Frederick Engels: "'Without the slavery of antiquity, no modern socialism'" (p. 516). Slavery, by all accounts, is bad. Yet it is also the form of social organization upon which, out of which, from which, Marxist dreamers construct their utopias. Ironically, Marxists might say, an oppressive form of social organization can give rise to a better form. The oppressive one was bad, the opposite of the new form that is good. Nonetheless, the bad and the good work together. As a kindly aunt might say: make lemonade out of lemons. Her metaphor is decidedly ironic. We can take something sour, something unpleasant to eat, and turn it into something that is pleasurable, a relief on hot days.

Indeed, from the perspective of some racists in the United States, Dr. Martin Luther King, Jr. can be seen as an ironic figure. In Dr. King we see a man who not only was a Christian minister but the holder of a Ph.D. from a major American research institution: Boston University. Insofar as racism often was supported by Christianity, Dr. King ironically used the religion of the master race to call for racial equality. So, too, he used his doctoral level education, earned at a bastion of the white race, to call for racial equality.

❖ *Exercise 1.7*

What follows is a section of the back cover copy of Elie Wiesel's novel, *Dawn* (1970). Locate and name the irony. Then, name and discuss the worldview(s) from which the irony emerges, which the irony supports.

> Through the night two men wait to look on the face of death. One of them is John Dawson, a British hostage. The other is Elisha, a young

Jew, a survivor of the Nazi death camps who has seen death close-up—but only as a victim. Elisha will be John Dawson's executioner.

❖ *Exercise 1.8*

Exercise 1.7 asked you to work analytically, to study the ways in which the cover copy writer used irony to describe the book. This exercise asks you to work constructively, to use irony actively to create your own composition. The constructive task:

Choose one of the flashpoints about which this book is concerned. Construct a question that cannot be answered with either "yes" or "no." Answer this question in a passage of two paragraphs. As you develop your answer, do so ironically: use the opposite of what you mean to reveal what you mean.

A Preview

Each of the following chapters will center around a particular flashpoint—race, class, gender, the environment, and war, respectively. At the center of each chapter resides a single text or small set of texts that speaks to the flashpoint: three editorials titled "Education" written by W.E.B. Du Bois; an excerpt from the American Roman Catholic Bishops' pastoral letter, *Economic Justice for All*; Sojourner Truth's speech, "A'n't I a Woman?"; Gary Snyder's poems "For All" and "Breasts"; and President Abraham Lincoln's "Second Inaugural Address." These texts not only particularize the flashpoints, but they are also all masterful demonstrations of the ways in which we figure and refigure issues of enduring human concern—issues that are at times glowing hot, at times ablaze, but always incendiary.

2

Figuring Race

Race as Symbolic Construct and Material Reality

Cornel West relays to his readers a powerful story in the introduction to *Race Matters,* his national best-seller (1993). Then a professor at Princeton University, Dr. West tells of a time when he and his wife traveled to New York City, he for a photoshoot for the book's cover, she for an appointment near Lexington and Park avenues. After he took his wife to her appointment, he parked his "rather elegant" car in a "safe" parking lot and waited for a cab (p. xv). He waited and waited as empty cab after empty cab passed him by. Finally, the tenth cab stopped, but not for him. It stopped instead for a "kind, well-dressed, smiling female fellow citizen of European descent" (p. xv). She confirmed his interpretation of the situation when she turned to him and said, "'this is really rather ridiculous, is it not?'" (p. xv).

She was referring, of course, to the racism to which Dr. West had been subjected. Cab after cab passed him by not because the taxi drivers did not need the fare. They passed him by because they did not need— or rather, want—the fare from a man of black African descent.

Later, after a successful photoshoot in which the photographer and book designer—both of white European descent—demonstrated their "expertise and enthusiasm," West met his wife again (p. xvi). They talked of their "fantasy" of moving to live in Addis Ababa, Ethiopia, the home of Dr. West's wife and the site of their wedding. Later, they relaxed at Sweetwater's, where the "ugly memories faded in the face of soulful music, soulful food, and soulful folk" (p. xvi). Finally, they returned home to Princeton, listening to "the soothing black music of Van Harper's Quiet Storm on WBLS 107.5," and "talked about what *race* matters have meant to the American past and of how much race *matters* in the American present" (p. xvi).

Dr. West's tale—coming as it does from one of America's preeminent intellectuals—indicates the ways in which race is both a "symbolic construct" and a "material reality." The phrase "symbolic construct" connotes ideas, words, images, and forms that might, or might not, manifest themselves in material form outside of symbolic activity. Consider Mickey Mouse, for instance. As a symbolic construct, Mickey Mouse is nearly omnipresent in America culture. He appears in cartoons, in movies, on the streets of Disney Land and Disney World. Yet, he appears only as a symbolic construct: he is artifice through and through. This is not to denigrate the figure of Mickey Mouse. Indeed, artifice is a good and necessary part of human life. Still, Mickey Mouse is not materially real. Even when he appears on the streets of Disney Land and Disney World, he appears as a costume. A human being refigures himself or herself to appear as Mickey Mouse: a living metaphor.

Still, many symbolic constructs are made manifest in material reality. Take a house. At one point, a house exists only as a symbolic construct. The architect, the builder, and the client all share a vision of the house, the house that does not exist except for in the form of these visions. When the house is built, however, it takes on a materially real form: it is no longer only a vision. Neither, however, is it an impersonation. The house, unlike Mickey Mouse, has integrity: it is itself.

The phrase "material reality," then, connotes things that exist in material form, though they might be the act of artifice. These things might, or might not, have an explicitly detailed concept behind them. The house does: it exists on paper, at least. Does a tree? This is a question that has driven human thought for eons. A tree is real, certainly: humans name it, touch it, sit under it, cut it. So too one can presume that even if humans weren't here, other flora or fauna would have relationships with the tree: it exists in the world. Whether or not there is an "ideal form" that exists eternally, an "ideal form" that gave rise to the tree, is a fascinating question, but one not to be considered at length here.

The general point is this: the flashpoints around which this book is moving, into which this book is delving, from which this book is emerging, exist both as symbolic constructs and as material realities. Race, the flashpoint of this chapter, is a symbolic construct, but not only that. It is a material reality, but not only that. It is both and must be considered as such, lest one miss its complexities and thus reduce it.

Consider again the passage from West's book, *Race Matters*. Dr. West points to the ways in which race is both a symbolic construct and a material reality. Consider these points:

1. He was left stranded by cab after cab, because he is of black African descent.

2. He found sympathy from a woman of white European descent, because she too saw the racism inherent in the scene.

3. He and his wife dream of moving to Addis Ababa, Ethiopia.

4. He and his wife relaxed in Sweetwater's.

5. He and his wife listened to "black" music on the drive back to Princeton.

Point #1 is the tale of an event that is materially real: cabs passed him by. Yet, the action of the cabdrivers is rooted in a symbolic construct. They saw standing on the street corner not one of America's pre-eminent intellectuals who is also a man of black African descent, but a man of black African descent, period. Symbolically, this means that Dr. West is dangerous, not to be taken on as a fare. They see a black man and they think, "danger."

Point #2 likewise reveals the interplay of race as symbolic construct and material reality. The cabdriver accepts the woman as a fare because, presumably, she is white. It doesn't matter that she is well-dressed, even though Dr. West mentions this. He is also well-dressed: in his trademark three-piece suit. If the cabdrivers were making a decision based on socioeconomic status, certainly Dr. West would have qualified, if clothes make the man. They don't, at least in this case. The cabdrivers are working here not on socioeconomic indicators but on racial. The cabdriver sees a white woman and thinks, "safe." She herself recognizes this fact in the tale, since she acknowledges to Dr. West the fact that the situation is ludricous.

Point #3 points to a highly symbolic moment, albeit one rooted in material reality. At the end of the day, Dr. West and his wife dream of Addis Ababa, of Ethiopia, of Africa. Like many Americans of black African descent, in the face of continuing American racism, they look to the "homeland." They think of Africa as a place where the division between whites and blacks is not an issue, or, if it is, it is only conceptual and not socially real. This dream, however, is manifestly conceptual, by definition: it is a dream. They haven't moved to Ethiopia, they only conceive of the possibility of such a move, a possibility desired because of the conceptual socially real racism of America.

As an interim step, perhaps, the couple goes to Sweetwater's. Although never explicitly identified as such, it can be inferred from Dr. West's description that Sweetwater's is an establishment that caters to, and is frequented by, African Americans. Dr. West claims that it is a place "of soulful music, soulful food, and soulful folk." "Soulful," without doubt, is a metaphor for things African American. Sweetwater's is an establishment that simultaneously creates a conceptual and socially real retreat from the white world. African Americans like Dr. West and his wife can enter this soulful world and remove themselves, at least temporarily, from the racist streets of Manhattan.

Even as they travel back to Princeton, however, the couple is able to maintain its protective shield. As they drive, they listen to "the soothing black music of Van Harper's Quiet Storm on WBLS 107.5." The adjectival phrase "black music" is a fascinating construction because it is precisely that. Certainly, the word "black" cannot mean color literally, because music cannot be any color, literally. If not literal, what trope is it? It is not ironic, for then it would really be white music. Given then racist events of the day, and the couple's dreams of Africa and enjoyment of Sweetwater's, it is difficult to imagine that they would find white music soothing. It is not analogy because there are no analogical pairs. I suggest that the phrase is a synecdoche.

As a synecdoche, it is a symbolic construct that attempts to create a worldview that counters the socially real racism that Dr. West faced. He understands this music to be "black" music, meaning that it is a representative part of a larger whole: "black culture." In listening to it, he listens to black culture, to the productive and creative possibilities and realities of folk of black African descent. In listening to this music, in naming "black music," Dr. West is creating a worldview in which African Americans can, in fact, create a world that counters the racist world in which Dr. West found himself in that day. This, without doubt, resonates with his dinner at Sweetwater's, his dreams of Africa: he is constructing, at least symbolically, of a world of black power, black possibility, black reality. Dr. West never falls prey to the racist division of white oppressor/black oppressed from which Malcolm X found himself emerging. However, Dr. West also recognizes, as does Malcolm X, that race is both symbolic construct and material reality. People look at him, certain concepts in mind, and act accordingly. He acts in turn, creating and dreaming other concepts and realities.

A passage from *The Autobiography of Malcolm X* (1993) also demonstrates how race is both a symbolic construct and a material reality. This section details Malcolm X's thoughts about his *Hajj*, his pilgrimmage to Mecca. To his surprise, early in his trip he is offered the use of a suite of rooms, a suite belonging to a male relative of the Saudi Arabian ruling family. The man, according to Malcolm X, "would have been considered 'white' in America" (p. 340). Moreover, this man had nothing to gain from offering his suite to Malcolm X. Malcolm X was relatively poor and a pariah in America. Whites distrusted him because of his work for the Nation of Islam, and he and the Nation of Islam had come to a parting of the ways. Malcolm X was adrift, searching for a new direction in Saudi Arabia. Still, in what was interpreted by Malcolm X as a selfless gift, the man gave him the rooms. This, Malcolm X writes, "was the start of a radical alteration in my whole outlook about 'white' men" (p. 340). This passage reveals part of the alteration:

> That morning was when I first began to reappraise the "white man." It was when I first began to perceive that "white man," as commonly used, means complexion only secondarily; primarily it described attitudes and actions. In America, "white man" meant specific attitudes and actions toward the black man, and toward all other non-white men. But in the Muslim world, I had seen that men with white complexions were more genuinely brotherly than anyone else had ever been. (p. 340)

Conceptually, Malcolm X undergoes a shift. He says that this man's gift of the suite forced him to reconceive the phrase "white man." As a black American, Malcolm X had linked skin complexion with attitude and action. "White man" connoted a certain sort of person, a person of "light" skin complexion who oppresses people of "dark complexion." Here, symbolic construct and material reality lead to a division between whites on one side and blacks on the other: whites oppress blacks; blacks are oppressed by whites. Conceptually, then, the phrase "white man" means oppressor; the phrase "black man" means oppressed. The Nation of Islam, as readers of *The Autobiography of Malcolm X* know, had constructed a religious mythology meant to name this division and overturn it: that of Yacub and his descendants (p. 167–171).

Malcolm X is shocked to discover that the material reality of Orthodox Islam does not match the concept of "white man" that he brought with him on the *Hajj*. Through the man's gift of the suite, and other events on his trip to Mecca, Malcolm X is forced to change his concept of "white man." No longer is he able to divide the world neatly between "white oppressors" and "black oppressed"; between "white devils" and "black angels"; between "white tyrants" and "black freedom-fighters." On the Hajj, Malcolm X encounters a material reality—that of harmony between people of different skin colors under the banner of Islam—that indicates his concepts are limited, indeed racist (p. 340). Not surprisingly, Malcolm X's entire worldview begins to change: he can no longer think of white people *per se* as the devil.

However, there is a tendency among Americans to ignore the question of race, either because it is a flashpoint to which they would rather close their eyes, or because it is a flashpoint that they think was extinguished by the Civil Rights movement of the 1960s. In some ways, this is true: one no longer finds publicly segregated bathrooms, for instance. Nor does one find urban transportation systems that force African Americans to the back of the bus, reserving the front seats for European Americans. Nonetheless, race is still a flashpoint refigured by language as only a cursory glance at contemporary life in America demonstrates. Consider, for instance, these incidents:

- A Korean-American woman, walking down a sidewalk in her Chicago neighborhood, is accosted by several African-American teenage men, driving past her in a car. They yell pseudo-Chinese language at her: "eenow," "feng-ho," and the like. These young men have mistaken this young woman as part of the wrong whole: they see someone who is "oriental" and think "Chinese."

- A European-American man, speaking to a friend who is a Lakota Sioux, claims that there never has been a foreign war fought on American soil. The Lakota Sioux shakes his head, smiles grimly. "How about the wars of European-American aggression against the native tribes?" At contest here is the word "war." What is its literal meaning? Its metaphoric? Its ironic? Were the battles against the native tribes not war?

The following exercise might help you to explore the ways in which race is a flashpoint figured and refigured by language that supports, and challenges, worldviews.

❖ *Exercise 2.1*

1. Consider three types of racial groups in America (e.g., white, black, latino). For each group, list as many derogatory slang words as you can. Then, ask yourself these two questions: Are any of these tropes? What is the worldview revealed by these words? Finally, interview two people. Ask them the following questions, and others you might compose: Have you heard these words used? When? By whom? What do you think the use of these words shows?

2. Many critics of television and film claim that European Americans dominate these art forms in this way: most television shows and films are about European-American families and people, and thus feature European-American actors. This is despite the demographic movement that will make European Americans a racial minority in the very near future. Furthermore, when non-European Americans are featured, they are often featured as criminals, as poor people, as dangerous in some way. Test these claims. Watch two nights of television shows. Consider these questions: What is the proportion of European-American actors to non-European-American actors? What types of people and situations do non-European-American actors depict? Do you notice any particular tropes used by the characters to refer to members of other races? What worldviews are implied by these tropes?

3. Consider the words "black," "white," "brown," "yellow," and "red." These are words that often are used to describe the racial features of people in America. For example, Native Americans often are referred to as having red skin. Using the *Oxford English Dictionary*, study the definitions of these words. Are they negative or positive? Do any of the definitions include metaphor? Analogy? Irony? Synecdoche? What are the worldviews implied in these definitions? Given the range of definitions, what effect might these words have on our worldviews when we use them to describe other humans?

It is true, on one hand, that we have come a long way since the NAACP lawyers and Brown v. Board of Education, since Rosa Parks and the bus boycott, since Martin Luther King, Jr., and the March on Washington. It is equally true, on the other, that race is still a flashpoint. No one knew this better than W.E.B. Du Bois, one of the founders of the NAACP and founding editor of its magazine, *The Crisis*. Included in Appendix A are three editorials from *The Crisis*, each written by Du Bois. Although they first appeared well over 75 years ago—in 1913, 1915, and 1922—they well indicate the ways in which race was, and is, a flashpoint, a flashpoint figured and refigured by language that challenges, and is challenged by, certain worldviews.

W.E.B. Du Bois and *The Crisis*

W.E.B. Du Bois, one of the first African Americans to earn a Ph.D. at Harvard University, was one of the greatest intellectual figures of the twentieth century. Scholar, journalist, editor, professor, activist: few people can claim even two of these titles, let alone all of them. Few, as well, can claim to have lived these titles with any of the expertise and success with which Du Bois lived them. As editor of *The Crisis*, for over twenty years Du Bois shaped it into an extremely powerful voice in the debate about race in the United States. Although Du Bois is best known for works like *The Souls of Black Folk*, the editorials in *The Crisis* offer students of figurative language a unique vantage, as many scholars have noted. Circulation numbers alone make them important. At its peak by the end of World War I, the magazine's subscription base totaled one hundred thousand. Thus, Du Bois' voice, and the other voices included in *The Crisis*, played no small, or ineloquent, part in the public discourse about race.

Consider, for example, the first of the editorials in the Appendix A: "Education," dated June, 1912. As an intellectual and activist, Du Bois was concerned about education in general, but education for African Americans in particular. The early part of the twentieth century was a period of tremendous growth in the theory and practice of public and private education. Du Bois' great contemporary, John Dewey, was actively at work in this same period. Du Bois understood that education was central to human life, and that education was central to the struggle about race. For his part, Du Bois argued that education—properly understood—was a means by which African Americans could overcome racism. White America understood this as well, according to Du Bois. For that reason, white America tended to argue that educating African Americans was not a good goal.

Du Bois, in this editorial, argues that education is not simply vocational training. As he says,

> . . .a training simply in technique will not do because general intelligence is needed for any trade, and the technique of trades changes.
>
> Indeed, by the careful training of intelligence and ability, civilization is continually getting rid of the hardest and most exhausting toil, and giving it over to machines, leaving human beings freer for higher pursuits and self-development.

Included in this passage are two implicit analogies and an explicit metaphor, both of which support and challenge both particular religious and political worldviews. The implicit analogy is found in this phrase: "civilization is continually getting rid of the hardest and most exhausting toil." This phrase resonates with one of the oldest of western stories: the expulsion of Adam and Eve from the Garden of Eden. Prior to the expulsion, Adam and Eve lived a work-free life, apparently. Or, if they did work it was toil-less: it was pleasure, not a burden. After the expulsion, Adam and Eve were condemned to a life of toil: Adam, Eve, and all humans were condemned to live by the sweat of their brows.

Du Bois, however, recognizes that the history of human civilization can be read as an attempt to mitigate this condemnation, to overcome the burden God bestowed upon humans. Thus, the first analogy:

Adam		Machines
———	as	———
Fall		Contemporary World

Civilization, more and more, is turning machines into Adam after the expulsion from the Garden. For centuries, Adam's descendants had to be Adam: they, too, were condemned to toil-full work, living by the sweat of their brow. However, the centuries have also seen the analogical displacement of machines for Adam. These human creations more and more are the Adam. Humans are freed, Du Bois claims, for "higher pursuits." Thus, the second analogy and the metaphor:

Adam		Contemporary Humans
———	as	———————————
Toil-Full Work		Higher Pursuits, Self-Development

This is to say, contemporary humans have the opportunity to be Adam's negative analogue. We cannot be Adam because we have machines. Adam was condemned to live his life in a base, material way, toiling simply to survive. Contemporary humans, because of the advance of civilization, have been able to escape God's wrath. With machines, humans have freed themselves more and more from Adam's toil. They are freer for "higher pursuits."

Implied in this scheme is the following analogy, perhaps. Like Adam in the garden, contemporary humans to be freed for higher pursuits.

Adam		Contemporary Humans
———	as	———
Garden		Contemporary World

It is not the case that toil-full work has been negated. Indeed, ditches need to be dug, fields need to be plowed, laundry needs to be washed. However, machines now have taken, to a certain extent at least, Adam's place. This is easily imagined: we in the United States no longer beat clothes on river rocks in order to wash them. We simply throw them into the machine, which washes them for us. Presumably, the time and energy saved can be devoted to endeavors other than toil-full work. The time and energy can be devoted to higher pursuits.

This, then, is the metaphor at the center of the analogical world that Du Bois is constructing: higher pursuits. It is metaphorical, in one way, because of its comparative adjective, "higher." Is any pursuit literally higher than any other? Only if the pursuit literally involves climbing mountains, flying airplanes, walking on tightropes, and the like. "Higher," as Du Bois uses it, indicates a value attached to the pursuit: it is better to pursue some things more than it is to pursue others.

"Better" is attached to higher, just as "worse" is attached to "lower." Consider, for instance, tracking in schools. The "best" students are in the highest track, just as the "worst" students are in the lowest. So, too, the prophet Moses, in the book of Genesis, traveled high on a mountain to receive the Ten Commandments. He did not travel low, beneath the Earth. Why not? Because that is the place of death. Indeed, as Greek mythology has it, Hades lives in the underworld. Although Hades is a brother of Zeus, and thus by rights could sit high on Mt. Olympus with the other Gods in the ancient Greek pantheon, his place is low, beneath the surface of the earth itself. Why? Because Hades is the God of death, of darkness.

Yet, the word "higher" is not the only metaphor in the phrase "higher pursuits." "Pursuits" itself is a metaphor: It points to the chase. Consider, for example, college education. One might say that "I am pursuing my B.S. in elementary education." The verb "pursuing" suggests that the B.A. is running away, or hiding, from the "I" of the sentence. It is as if the degree is the prey, the degree earner the predator. Or, the degree is the hunted, and the degree earner the hunter. Can one literally pursue a degree? No. However, one can metaphorically: the act of earning the degree might well seem like a chase, a hunt. The degree earner might need to use all her cunning and skill to bag the game because the game is wily, smart, strong.

Du Bois, then, is deeply involved in a figurative world. This figurative world supports particular worldviews, and challenges others. Among the worlds it challenges are these:

   a. A worldview that accepts God's condemnation of Adam to a life of toil-full work.

b. A worldview that emphasizes practical skills training for African Americans rather than higher-level education.

It would replace these with two others:

aa. A worldview that holds that humans can overcome God's condemnation.

bb. A worldview that holds that African Americans, like white European Americans, should pursue what Du Bois calls "the broadest and highest education possible."

The first, "a" versus "aa," has been discussed previously at length. The second, "b" against "bb," places Du Bois squarely against another African-American titan: Booker T. Washington. Washington, for his part, argued that the best way for African Americans to overcome racial barriers in post–Civil War America was to train in the so-called "practical arts": machinery, farming, carpentry, and the like. This, so the argument goes, would permit African Americans to earn much needed money and thus establish gainful, and independent, lives. Although Du Bois does not denigrate the "practical arts," he argues that African Americans must develop themselves as intellectuals as well. To do otherwise is to remain like Adam, tied to toil-full work. As he says in the editorial, the "end of education" is not the thing, but the child. Practical skills education focuses too much, he asserts, on the thing to be produced. We train carpenters, for instance, because we want the thing that carpenters build. In this scenario, the human is placed second to the thing the human produces. Du Bois argues as well that to accept training in the practical arts as the epitome of education is to remain forever a class of laborers, second, always, to those who control the use of labor.

Here is the irony, implied by Du Bois, but nonetheless present: African Americans are freed from slavery but, as laborers, are forever slaves to the people who use their labor. In short, Du Bois fears that African Americans have been "freed" to a life bound by a caste system: they have been freed not to equality, but to a subordinate status. The European Americans, as Du Bois says, "want caste; a place for everybody and everybody in his father's place with themselves on top, and 'Niggers' at the bottom where they belong."

Analysis: Du Bois on Education

This section provides you the opportunity to engage in your own analytic study of W.E.B. Du Bois' editorials on education and race as they appeared in the pages of *The Crisis*. Appendix A includes three editorials, all titled "Education," but from different years: 1912, 1915, and 1922, respectively.

❖ *Exercise 2.2: Sentences*

Consider the following five sentences, all drawn from the texts included in Appendix A. For each sentence, mark the tropes that are present. What kind are they? How do they work? Are they effective? As you answer these questions, attend to the worldviews that the tropes support and challenge.

1. To them [those who emphasize the training of laborers] Indianapolis exists for the sake of its factories and not the factories for the sake of Indianapolis. (1912)

2. . . .the despising of men is growing and the caste spirit is rampant in the land; it is laying hold of the public schools and it has the colored public schools by the throat, North, East, South, and West. (1912)

3. The quiet insidious persistent attempt to keep the mass of the Negroes in America in just sufficient ignorance to render them incapable of realizing their power or resisting the position of inferiority into which the bulk of the nation is determined to thrust them was never stronger than today. (1915)

4. Is there any justice in making a particular body of men the drudges of society, destined for the worst work under the worst conditions and at the lowest pay, simply because a majority of their fellow men for more or less indefinite and superficial reasons do not like them? (1915).

5. There is a widespread feeling that a school is a machine. (1922)

❖ Exercise 2.3: Sections

Consider one section from each editorial, summarized in the following list. For each section, mark the tropes that are present. What kind are they? How do they work? Are they effective? As you answer these questions, attend to the worldviews that the tropes support and challenge.

1. Two paragraphs of "Education," 1912. The first paragraph begins with "The first flaw" and the second with "When the proud." Here Du Bois is beginning to detail his criticism of dominant theories and practices of education.

2. The section of "Education," 1915, titled "The Basic Fallacy." Here Du Bois attempts to expose the problems with any argument that suggests that (a) The object of life is work, and (b) "Negroes" are meant to be workers.

3. The first three paragraphs of "Education," 1922. Here Du Bois lays out a fundamental problem. Schools are criticized because they seem to be like factories. Yet, African-American parents, according to Du Bois, do not know how terrible the schools are.

❖ Exercise 2.4: Topics

Consider the following three tasks, each of which ask you to focus on one of the entire editorials included in Appendix A.

1. Consider one of the editorials. In a 500–750 word letter to Du Bois, attend to the following questions: Which metaphor (or analogy, or synecdoche) is primary? This is to say, of all those used in the Du Bois editorial, which is the most central to the text, the one without which the text could not survive? What is the worldview that this metaphor supports? What is the worldview that it challenges?

2. Consider the excerpt as a whole. In a 3–4 page letter to Du Bois, attend to the following questions: With which metaphor (or analogy, or synecdoche) would you describe one of the editorials? This should be your own metaphor, not one drawn from the text. Why this metaphor?

What is the worldview that it supports? What is the worldview that it challenges? Does this metaphor indicate that you disagree with Du Bois? If so, why do you disagree? Does it indicate that you agree with Du Bois? If so, why do you agree?

❖ Exercise 2.5: Figuring Race

This exercise asks you to become an editorialist on the topic of race. Each task requires you to take on a different guise, conduct different research. The point of each, however, is to require you to think of yourself as a member of a particular community that you want to move into a new understanding of the issue of race in America. Use Du Bois' editorials as a model for your own editorials in the following ways:

- Provide a title for each.
- For task one, use short paragraphs, mimicking Du Bois' practice in the 1912 editorial.
- For task two, use section headers in order to indicate shifts in topics and argument, mimicking Du Bois' practice in the 1915 editorial.
- Consciously attend to the use of metaphor, analogy, synecdoche, irony. Attend also to race as it informs both topics.

1. Imagine that you have been asked to compose a 500–750 word guest editorial for your town newspaper that addresses Du Bois' claim in his 1922 editorial that "there is a widespread feeling that a school is a machine." Agree or disagree with Du Bois. In your editorial, draw on your own experience. In addition, draw on the results of field work that you have performed. With the permission of school officials, observe an elementary school for a day: see if, indeed, it looks like a machine.

2. Imagine that you have taken a position on the editorial staff of a regional newspaper. The newspaper plans a series of articles on this question: How are schools preparing their students for the workforce? You have been asked to write a 750–1000 word editorial that answers this question. Having studied Du Bois, you have this question in mind:

Is the primary purpose of a school to service area businesses, or is the primary purpose of the school to service the growth and development of its students as humans, independent of race and of the needs of the region's businesses? As you prepare to write this, interview a teacher and a business person. Ask them to reflect on Du Bois' belief that training for careers is secondary to "higher pursuits and self-development."

3

Figuring Class

Class as Symbolic Construct and Material Reality

Nowhere has class been more forcefully discussed than in the pages of *The Communist Manifesto*. No one has discussed class with as much clarity and vigor than Karl Marx in those pages. This is not to say that *The Communist Manifesto* is unchallengeable, nor is it to say that Karl Marx has had the final say on this flashpoint. Nonetheless, *The Communist Manifesto* and Marx, for better or worse, initiated and have, to a great extent, defined the boundaries of the conversation.

Written in 1848, *The Communist Manifesto* (1992) is, literally, a manifesto. It is not a philosophical treatise, though certainly it is informed by the philosophic tradition. *The Communist Manifesto* is, rather, a call to action, written first and foremost for the members of the Communist Party. Its secondary audience is the rest of the "workers of the world." With its famous last lines, it calls them to unite against the oppressive bourgeoisie and the industrial regime: the workers, Marx claims, have nothing to lose but their chains (p. 58).

This famous closing call is, without doubt, metaphorical. Workers in industrial Europe literally were not chained to their machines, chained to the factories in which the machines were housed, chained to the towns and cities in which the factories had been built. They were not slaves, at least literally. Rather, Marx uses the metaphor "chains" to indicate a worldview. Within this world are, essentially, two classes: the bourgeoisie on one hand, the proletariat on the other.

According to Marx, the bourgeoisie own the industrial order's productive capital: they own the factories, the shipyards, and the mills. They are relatively few in number, but strong in social, economic, and political power. The proletariat are many in number, but weak in social, economic, and political power. They are not the owners, but the workers. They are the ones hired by the bourgeoisie to operate the machines in the factories, to build the ships, to melt and shape the metal, to cut and trim the wood. The only power that they have is their labor: they sell themselves to earn money so that they might buy food, clothes, shelter—so that, in a word, they might live.

At the heart of the struggle is this: the bourgeoisie want to pay the proletariat as little as they are able for at least two reasons. First, the bourgeoisie want to make as much profit as possible. The more money they pay to the proletariat, the less profit they make. Second, they want to keep the proletariat stationary and powerless. If, in capitalist society, money brings mobility and power, the bourgeoisie want the proletariat to have neither of these because either might disrupt the industrial order. As Marx sees it, the bourgeoisie want to pay the proletariat just enough to keep it alive so that it can continue to work for the bourgeoisie. If the proletariat make too much money, it will begin to make possible for itself a life outside the factories and, even, want to become an owner of capital itself. These then are the chains in which the workers of the world are kept: wages. The workers make only enough to live, but not enough to live better. While the bourgeoisie construct mansions with the money brought to it through the labor of the workers, the workers, especially in Marx's era, built hovels. While the bourgeoisie purchase silken robes with money brought to it through the labor of the workers, the workers, especially in Marx's era, wore coarse garments. While the bourgeoisie procure the choicest foods with money brought to it through the labor of the workers, the workers, especially in Marx's era, ate much less well, to say the least.

Class, as seen through the pages of *The Communist Manifesto*, is a symbolic construct in which slavery is the true order. The bourgeoisie own not simply capital, but humans and their labor. The workers own nothing. Moreover, in selling their labor, they sell themselves: they are trapped in an order from which escape is difficult, at best.

Literally, to be sure, the proletariat in the nascent industrial democracies of Marx's Europe were not slaves, nor were the bourgeoisie slave owners. Yet the material reality of the relationship between these two classes was bad enough to warrant the metaphor: the squalor and oppressive conditions of the factories, the shipyards, the mills have been well-documented. One need not be a Marxist or a communist to recognize this.

A close reading of *The Communist Manifesto*, then, reveals class as both a symbolic construct and a material reality. Many texts in the post-*Manifesto* era also open to their readers both dimensions of class: Steinbeck's *Grapes of Wrath*, Veblen's *Theory of the Leisure Class*, and Terkel's *Working*, to name three. So, too, a short story by James Baldwin, "Previous Condition" (*Going to Meet the Man*, 1998) offers its readers a way to understand class as a symbolic construct and a material reality. This short story is particularly worthy of discussion because it shows the ways in which race and class intertwine, often obscuring each from the other.

"Previous Condition" concerns an African-American actor named Peter, a man who has no home, both literally and metaphorically. His best friend is a Jewish man, Jules Weissman. His lover is a white, married woman of European descent, Ida. At one point in the story, Peter reflects on the nomadic nature of his adult life. As he says, he had "done a lot of traveling in my time" (p. 85). This leads him to reflect on the "old shack" in which he was raised. It was, Peter says, one of "the kind of houses colored people live in all over the U.S." It was also located in the "nigger part of town" (p. 85).

Peter here intertwines race and class, an intertwining that bedevils him for the rest of the story, causing conflict with both his mother and his lover. He recognizes that he was raised in an "old shack," a description carrying with it the unmistakable mark of class anxiety and embarrassment. As a "shack," this dwelling has an implied series of oppositions, ranging from house to mansion. Peter, then, sees his childhood as marked by class: he was poor.

Not only was he poor, however. He was also a "nigger," a "colored" person, an African American. Although his mother and lover will disagree with him, he connects the "fact" of his race with his class condition, he connects the "fact" of being African American with the class condition of all African Americans. First, he says that his shack was in the "nigger part of town." This is a synecdoche with analogical implications. The synecdoche is this: the whole—the town—has a least two parts: the "nigger" part and, presumably, the "white" part. The analogical implication is this:

Shacks		Houses
———	as	———
"Nigger" Part of Town		"White" Part of Town

This synecdoche and analogy extend throughout the United States. Just as the "nigger" part is to the town, so, too, the town is to the United States. He claims that his house was the kind of house "colored people live in all over the U.S." Thus:

"Nigger" Part		Town
———	as	——
Town		Country

This synecdoche and analogy is confirmed at another point in the story, when Peter is kicked out of an apartment. A nice place located in a "white" neighborhood, the apartment was rented for him, in his name, by his friend, Jules. When the landlady discovers that Peter is, in fact, African American, she tosses him on the street: "I got the right to know who's in my house! This is a white neighborhood, I don't rent to colored people. Why don't you on uptown, like you belong" (p. 91)? In short, his attempt to live in a comfortable, affordable place—to enter the land of a higher class—is thwarted because he is "colored."

Throughout all this is another analogy, an analogy that links race and class. Peter suggests in his various tales that

Black Americans		White Americans
———	as	———
Poverty		Wealth

As Peter says, he lived in a "shack," which is "the kind of houses colored people live in all over the U.S."

His mother, however, refuses to abide by this analogy, by this suggestion that race and class are inexorable partners, that whites are of higher class, blacks of lower. At another point in the story, Peter recounts the first time he was called "nigger." As a child he came across a white playing with a ball, alone. He suggested that they play catch, but she said that "My mother don't let me play with niggers," and continued to hurl this epithet after him as he ran away: "Nigger, nigger, nigger" (p. 86)!

When he arrived home, he asked his mother what it meant. She brushed aside his question, telling him to "go wash your face... You dirty as sin" (p. 86). He came back washed, but not to her standards. She washes him herself and then berates him: "You run around dirty like you do all the time, everybody'll call you a little nigger, you hear?"

Later, more tenderly, she tells him

> "Baby, don't fret. Next time somebody calls you nigger you tell them you'd rather be your color than be lowdown and nasty like some white folks is." (pp. 86–7)

This sequence shows that Peter has misread his neighborhood, indeed his life, and that his mother refuses his incorrect analogy. Peter has misread his neighborhood because at least one white family lives there: witness the white girl. If, indeed, Peter's childhood neighborhood was poor, then this white family must be poor as well.

In addition, his mother suggests that he can and should distinguish between poor white people and poor black people. Indeed, she suggests that it is possible for African Americans to be a higher class of poor people when judged against poor whites: if he keeps himself clean and acts properly he will be better than the "lowdown and nasty" white people.

Moreover, his mother invokes a very old metaphor to help make her point: "dirty as sin." This metaphor implies an analogy, which many of us know, having heard it from our own mothers (and fathers):

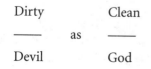

Dirty   Clean

———   as   ———

Devil   God

Peter's mother claims that his dirt is like sin. Insofar as she also contrasts her own sense of cleanliness with the dirtiness of some lowdown and nasty white folk, she implies that her own life is more Godly.

Like his mother, Peter's white lover, Ida, refuses Peter's analogical link between race and class. She refuses to see what is materially real—divisions between the races and classes—and symbolically constructs this reality in a way that doesn't match the reality that she sees and, we learn, the reality that she herself has experienced.

Peter tells us that

> Last year Ida took me driving in her big car and we passed through a couple of towns upstate. We passed some crumbling houses on the left. The clothes on the line were flying in the wind.
>
> "Are people living there?" asked Ida.
>
> "Just darkies," I said.
>
> Ida passed the car ahead, banging angrily on the horn. "D'you know you're becoming paranoiac, Peter?"
>
> "All right. All right. I know a lot of white people are starving too."
>
> "You're damn right they are. I know a little about poverty myself."
>
> (pp. 87–8)

We see in this passage that Peter, as an adult, sees the analogy very cleanly: white are to the upper class as "darkies" are to the lower class. The imprint of his own impoverished childhood, reinforced by experiences as an adult, compels him to view what is materially real—the fact of class divisions and poverty—through a particular symbolic construct. Ida, in contrast, sees the world much differently. As such, she has a different worldview than Peter. Where Peter sees an inexorable analogy connecting blackness and poverty, whiteness and wealth, Ida sees a more complex picture. White does not necessarily mean wealth, just as black does not necessarily mean poverty. This symbolic construction of class arises for Ida from her lived experienced: she knows "a little about poverty." As Peter himself admits, she "had come from the kind of family called shanty Irish" (p. 88).

Ida places herself into a world of poverty with the aid of synecdoche. The adjective "shanty" qualifies the noun, "Irish." This implies that other, similar adjectives can be used: house Irish, mansion Irish, and so forth. Her own part is the part that is poor. She is Irish—the whole—

but a part of the Irish that is distinct from other parts, more wealthy parts.

Her synecdoche also links her analogically to Peter, and thus to all poor African Americans. As a child, she was his class equal: if he was shack black, she was shanty Irish. The analogical schemes are these:

$$\frac{\text{Ida}}{\text{Shanty Irish}} \text{ as } \frac{\text{Peter}}{\text{Shack Blacks}}$$

And

$$\frac{\text{Shanty Irish}}{\text{Irish}} \text{ as } \frac{\text{Shack Blacks}}{\text{Blacks}}$$

Ida may well have been from the kind of family against whom Peter's mother had issued her warning: lowdown and nasty white folk. We learn that Ida had married for money, thereby raising herself from one class to another. As an adult, she was Peter's class superior, but she still carried with her the knowledge she had gained as a child.

That said, one might easily contest these past 11 pages with this comment: "Isn't this all just symbolic construct with no basis in material reality? Aren't these tales of class from books? Do they represent reality? Is any worker a slave, as Marx claims? Are there really shack blacks and shanty Irish, the way Baldwin describes them? Are there, really, classes in America? Isn't this so-called 'flashpoint' more of a dull glow?"

I could, of course, appeal to more studies and more books to make the case that class is both a symbolic construct and a material reality. This move, however, simply would lead the persistent critic to wonder, again, if this isn't just the phantasm of books, which are after all symbolic constructs in and of themselves. I could point to my own lived reality and ask questions like these: Is it a marker of class division that houses in a town near where I live sell, on the average, for over $300,000? Is it a marker of class division that these homes are large and beautiful surrounded by acres of fields and forests? Is it a marker of class division that homes in a neighborhood not 15 miles away are in disrepair, on small lots, and sell for much less? Is it a class marker that the schools serving the families who live in the town of expensive homes are markedly better than the schools serving the families who live in the neighborhood of inexpensive homes? Is it a marker of class division that the families who live in the town of expensive homes served by excellent schools tend to be very white collar professionals (physicians, attorneys, corporate leaders)? Is it a marker of class division that the families who live in the neighborhood of inexpensive homes served by troubled schools tend to be very blue collar (factory workers, service industry employees, and the like)? Why else do we have the metaphors "blue collar" and "white collar" than to distinguish between classes?

Rather than belabor this point, let me turn you to your own lives and ask you to study the ways in which class is figured and refigured through language.

❖ *Exercise 3.1*

1. Take a walk in the area that surrounds your campus. Work street by street. Note what you see: types of houses and their condition, types of cars and their condition, types of stores, restaurants, businesses, types of people, and the like. Once you have gathered these notes together, describe what you have observed and organize your descriptions into categories. Name the categories. Then, ask yourself these questions: What tropes have I used? What might these tropes say about the ways in which we figure and refigure "class"?

2. Impose on two or three friends. Ask these questions of them (and others you think are important): What is your family income? How many of your family members have graduated from college? What types of books do you or your family members read for fun? What television shows do they watch? In what sort of house were you raised? Attend in particular to the tropes that they use to answer these questions. Then, ask yourself this question: What might their answers say about the way that we figure and refigure "class"?

3. Think of your own hometown, your own home neighborhood. Describe it: sizes and types of homes, lots, cars, whether it is near any industry or businesses. Think of a nearby town or neighborhood that is markedly different. Describe it as well: sizes and types of homes, lots,

cars, whether it is near any industry or businesses. Attend to the tropes that you used to make these descriptions. Then ask yourself this question: What might these tropes say about the ways we figure and refigure "class"?

Whether you are a Marxist, a laissez-faire capitalist, a democratic socialist, or an economic pragmatist, you live a world marked by class and by class conflict. It is in this world that the American Catholic Bishops found themselves when they published their *Economic Justice for All: Pastoral Letter on Catholic Social Teaching and the U.S. Economy* (1986).

The American Catholic Bishops and *Economic Justice for All*

As a genre, the pastoral letter has a long tradition, dating back to the letters of St. Paul, which are included in the New Testament. These first letters were written to instruct, support, and cajole the early Christian communities in various locations: Corinth, Rome, Galatia, among them. St. Paul's self-proclaimed mission was to spread the good news of Jesus Christ to the Gentiles (the converts to Christianity) and used the genre of the pastoral letter, in addition to personal visits, to do so. The pastoral letter, at its origin, was meant to sustain the Christian community. However, St. Paul's letters also became part of wider public discourse. People outside the Christian community came to read them as well, simply to learn more about Christianity or to gather fuel for their fiery attacks on the religion or to gather faith as they converted.

The pastoral letter, then, has always had two functions. First, and foremost, it is written to a particular group of people: Christians until the Reformation (when Protestants split from Roman Catholicism) and Roman Catholics thereafter. Leaders of the faith use the letters as means of mass communication: the letter speaks to their communities when they are unable to do so personally. Whether intentionally or unintentionally, the pastoral letter also has a broader, albeit secondary, audience: people who are not part of the faith. Hence, Muslims may, and do, read St. Paul's letters. So, too, non-Roman Catholics, non-Christians, even atheists, may, and do, read *Economic Justice For All: Pastoral Letter on Catholic Social Teaching and the U.S. Economy*.

This pastoral letter is not written as a theological treatise: it does not instruct people on the mysteries of the Godhead. Rather, it applies theological priniciples to the economy: it instructs its readers how Roman Catholics—and by implication all faithful Christians—might work to establish an economic system that, as the title indicates, offers "justice for all." For students of figurative language, it is also an excellent example of the ways in which we figure and refigure class.

The title itself is the place to begin this analysis. What is "economic justice for all?" Although the pastoral letter goes to great lengths to discuss this, one can see immediately that the Bishops draw on a particular piece of American ritual to open their letter: the so-called "Pledge of Allegiance." Recited by school children around the country, it goes as follows:

> I pledge allegiance to the flag of the United States of America,
> And to the Republic for which it stands,
> One nation,
> Under God,
> With liberty and justice for All.

The Bishops, clearly, link their own efforts to the fundamental pledge, with this twist: they name economic justice as part of the overall phrase, "justice for all." The title of the pastoral letter, then, is a synecdoche.

As a noun, "justice" has an abstract meaning, applicable to many particular situations, events, and ideas. One might, for instance, speak of

Personal Justice

or

Family Justice

or

Pedagogical Justice

or

Criminal Justice

or

Administrative Justice

These phrases share two elements: the same noun and the same phrasal construction. "Justice" is common throughout and all are constructed with this typical pattern: adjective-noun. Justice, as the noun, is the whole. It is the abstract category. The adjectives mark parts of the whole: they begin to delineate what "justice" means by limiting its scope, by claiming it for particular spaces and places.

The U.S. Roman Catholic Bishops call for "economic justice" is simply, but bracingly, synecdoche. Part of the concept of "justice," they claim, is economic justice. One cannot fully understand the concept of justice, the title suggests, without looking at a particular part: economic justice.

I say that this is a "bracing" claim because the title is, potentially, ironic as well. One must wonder if the millions of adults who want millions of children to recite this phrase have any idea that a group like the Bishops would read "economic justice" into and out of the phrase "justice for all." Do these adults see, as the Bishops do, this American conundrum? While America "has provided an unprecedented standard of living for millions of people," it has also "left behind" many, those "sisters and brothers who are poor, unemployed, homeless, and living on the edge" (Section 10).

Although the Bishops work out of their faith in the God made manifest in Jesus Christ, they are not unlike Marx. They understand that the country is divided between the rich and the poor, the employed and unemployed, those with homes and those without, those at the center and those on the edge.

The Bishops concern themselves with economic justice because, finally, their worldview demands it. They do not operate out of a laissez-faire Darwinianism that would suggest that the strong will survive and that the weak, naturally, will perish. Rather, all people are their "sisters and brothers." Literally? Of course not. Metaphorically? Yes.

Why is it that all people, even the poor, the unemployed, the homeless, and the ones living on the edge are sisters and brothers to the Bishops? Why is it that the Bishops, in their call for economic justice, have pointed to the part of the American whole that many of us would rather ignore? They do so as followers of Jesus Christ. This is not the Jesus Christ who supports only the wealthy, the Jesus Christ who dines in mansions and on yachts. It is rather, the Jesus of the Parable of the Last Judgement. It is the Jesus who claimed that he is the one who hungers for food and thirsts for drink, that whenever people feed the hungry and give drink to the thirsty, they do, indeed, serve God (Section 4). This is a complex metaphor and analogy. Schematically, we can understand them like this:

Roman Catholics		Brothers and Sisters
———————————	as	———————————
Poor, Unemployed, Homeless, On the Edge		Brothers and Sisters

This is so, the Bishops claim, because of this analogy:

Jesus' Followers		Jesus' Followers
———————————	as	———————————
Hungry and Thirsty		Jesus

The Bishops claim, in essence, that contemporary Catholics must be concerned about economic life because Jesus was. Moreover, contemporary American Catholics are urged to claim the poor and impoverished as their own because Jesus himself claimed metaphorical identification with these people. Jesus didn't simply say that his followers should attend to the poor because he did: this is a powerful analogy, but not at heart of the Jesus' message, according the Bishops. Rather, Jesus claimed to be these people: feed them, he says, because in so doing, you feed me.

This is not to say, however, that the Bishops are Marxists: nothing could be further from the truth. First, as has been made clear, their worldview differs fundamentally with that of Marx: they are theists and he is not; they are Christians and he is not.

Second, the Bishops do not call for class war, for a "dictatorship of the proletariat," however temporary it might be. As the Bishops say, they are concerned about the dignity of all people, not simply the so-called "lower-class": "every economic decision and institution must be judged in light of whether it protects or undermines the dignity of the human person" (Section 13). That said, the Bishops are also clear in this statement: "all members of society have a special obligation to the poor and vulnerable" (Section 16).

Analysis: *Economic Justice for All*

This section provides you the opportunity to engage in your own analytic study of *Economic Justice for All: Pastoral Letter on Catholic Social Teaching and the U.S. Economy.* Appendix B includes the Preface of the letter.

❖ *Exercise 3.2: Sentences*

Consider the following five sentences, all drawn from the text included in Appendix B. For each sentence, mark the tropes that are present. What kind are they? How do they work? Are they effective? As you answer these questions, attend to the worldviews that the tropes support and challenge.

1. The pastoral letter is not a blueprint for the American economy. (Section 12)

2. The challenge for us is to discover in our own place and time what it means to be "poor in spirit." (Section 4)

3. Like family life, economic life is one of the chief areas where we live out our faith, love our neighbors, confront temptation, fulfill God's creative design, and achieve our holiness. (Section 6)

4. As *Americans*, we are grateful for the gift of freedom and committed to the dream of "liberty and justice for all." (Section 8)

5. We feel the pain of our sisters and brothers who are poor, unemployed, homeless, living on the edge. (Section 10)

❖ *Exercise 3.3: Sections*

Consider five sections of the letter, summarized in the following list. All are drawn from the text included in Appendix B. For each section, mark the tropes that are present. What kind are they? How do they work? Are they effective? As you answer these questions, attend to the worldviews that the tropes support and challenge.

1. Section 6. Here, the Bishops further their justification for writing the letter. They liken economic life to family life, and appeal to the dictates of the Second Vatican Council. This Council convened in the early 1960s with this goal: re-orienting Roman Catholicism to the demands of the modern world.

2. Section 18. Here, the Bishops discuss their views on the role of the government in economic life.

3. Section 1. Here, the Bishops establish why they, as Christian leaders, must address economic conditions.

4. Section 4. Here, the Bishops begin to lay the Biblical foundations for their work.

5. Section 16. Here the Bishops continue to root the themselves in the Bible with particular appeals to the Jewish and Christian Bibles.

❖ *Exercise 3.4: Topics*

Consider the following two tasks, both of which ask you to focus on the entire excerpt of the letter included in Appendix B. What kind are they? How do they work? Are they effective? As you answer these questions, attend to the worldviews that the tropes support and challenge.

1. Consider the excerpt as a whole. In a 3–4 page letter to your class, attend to the following questions: Which metaphor (or analogy, or synecdoche) is primary? This is to say, of all those used in the letter, which is the most central to the text, the one without which the text could not survive? What is the worldview that this metaphor supports? What is the worldview that it challenges?

2. Consider the excerpt as a whole. In a 3–4 page letter to the Bishops, attend to the following questions: With which metaphor (or analogy, or synecdoche) would you describe the excerpt? This should be

your own metaphor, not one drawn from the text. Why this metaphor? What is the worldview that it supports? What is the worldview that it challenges? Does this metaphor indicate that you disagree with the Bishops? If so, why do you disagree? Does it indicate that you agree with the Bishops? If so, why do you agree?

❖ *Exercise 3.5: Figuring Class*

The following exercise asks you to become letter writers on the topic of class, yourselves. Each task requires you to take on a different guise, and conduct different research. The point of each, however, is to require you to try to move a particular community into a new understanding of the issue of class in America. Use *Economic Justice for All* as a model for your letters in the following ways:

- Use **BOLD HEADERS** to separate distinct topics.
- Use running section numbers to separate paragraphs. This is to say, each paragraph should be numbered continuously from #1 to the final paragraph.
- Attend consciously to the use of tropes (metaphor, analogy, irony, synecdoche) in your text.

1. Imagine that you once belonged to a very tight-knit group in which music or movies were the most important foundational texts in the group's life. One of your parents used the following analogy to describe the importance of music or movies in your lives: "It is like the Bible to them." Your group has dispersed: some went to college, others to the military, others to work. You have encountered this flashpoint in your own life: class. Compose a 4–5 page letter addressed to all members of your group. You want to them to understand, and even agree with, your response to this line from the Bishop's letter: "economic decisions have human consequences and moral content (Section 1). Draw on a song (or songs) or a movie (or movies) with which your group is at least familiar in order to discuss your response. You need not agree with the Bishops.

2. Imagine that you have become a policy adviser to the governor of a state. This state is embroiled in an education funding crisis. By way of court order, poor school districts have forced the state to give them more money. The state must decide its position. It has these choices:

a. Pass a constitutional amendment that says that the state is not responsible for funding local school districts.

b. Institute an income tax. The proceeds would be distributed to school districts across the state. This would supplement the proceeds of property taxes, which are currently used to fund education. Poorer districts would receive more income-tax money than wealthier districts.

The governor has asked you conduct a focus group with five citizens. Choose five people that you can gather together for an hour, and ask them these questions: Which option, "a" or "b," do they prefer? Why? Then, write a letter to the governor's cabinet, outlining the results of the focus group and your own recommendations.

Draw on any sources that will help you.

4

Figuring Gender

Gender as Symbolic Construct and Material Reality

As a word, "gender" refers both to males and females, men and women, boys and girls. This obvious point was exposed brilliantly by the French philosopher Simone de Beauvoir, nearly fifty years ago. She writes in the introduction to her monumental work, *The Second Sex* (1974), that

> to go for a walk with one's eyes open is enough to demonstrate that humanity is divided into two classes of individuals whose clothes, faces, bodies, smiles, gaits, interests, and occupations are manifestly different. Perhaps these differences are superficial, perhaps they are destined to disappear. What is certain is that right now they do most obviously exist. (p. xvii)

Beauvoir's opening phrase has both literal and metaphorical dimensions. Literally, one might "go for a walk": one might stroll down a street, through an office and see the differences. Yet, Beauvoir also invites us to "go for a walk" with our minds open, not just our eyes. It is one thing to see, another to comprehend. "Eyes" here stands for the mind: open yourself, she suggests, to gender as it is constructed. You then will "see" what is there: gender difference.

To be sure, one might quibble with Beauvoir's point. For instance, Beauvoir writes that there are two kinds of people whose "occupations are manifestly different." We can say that this is changing. Women in America, for instance, now occupy jobs once closed to them—or severely limited—in great numbers. Witness, for one example, the number of physicians who are women. So, too, we have seen in clothing, in hairstyles, in body care, a greater crossing between "men" and "women." Singers like Michael Jackson and Boy George are particularly public examples of this: they have androgynous qualities that blur the distinctions between men and women. So, too, many men now wear earrings. Are they women? Not biologically. However, they now sport an affect that is still identified as female. Metaphorically, one might say that they are like females.

Nonetheless, Beauvoir's point is quite correct. We are divided between males and females, men and women, boys and girls. Consider, for instance, the locker rooms at a health club where my son has taken swimming lessons. A sign posted at the entrance to the men's locker rooms states this: "Girls 5+ years not allowed in the Men's Locker Room." The corresponding sign, referring to boys, is posted at the entrance to the women's locker room. The health club seems to be saying something like the following. Prior to five years of age, children are relatively unaware of the nuances of gender differences, and adults themselves don't view children of the opposite gender, under the age of five, as people from whom they need to hide their nakedness. However, at the age of five, gender differentiation occurs: children of this age and older neither should see the naked bodies of adults of the opposite gender, nor should their naked bodies be seen by adults of the opposite gender.

Why does Beauvoir take pains to make what is a seemingly obvious point, that males and females are different? She does so for two reasons. First, she wants to establish the terms of her argument: there are men and women, and she wants to write about women. Second, she writes in reaction to women thinkers and writers who, like herself, are concerned about gender. She claims that some, in their search for equality, too quickly want to erase the differences between men and women, want to become men. These thinkers, Beauvoir writes, attempt to address the flashpoint with a metaphorical magic wand: they will make it go away by claiming that there is no flashpoint at all, that they, as women, are men.

Beauvoir, in contrast, cleanly divides humanity into men and women and calls gender for what it is. Not only are there differences between the genders; there is tension as well, a tension borne of and by inequality. For eons, humans have constructed symbolic and material systems that place men in a position of superiority and women in a position of inferiority. For over one hundred years now, many women, and some men, have worked to subvert this order. I often remind my college students when this topic arises that women in America have had the right to vote only for 80 years, and only because many women, and some men, fought for years to bring this right about. Or, as I often remind my college students when this topic arises, the women we now see in the highest levels of the most powerful professions in the United States would not have been in these positions 50 years ago.

Not incidentally, the previous paragraph is rife with figurative language. Even as I myself write about this issue, I use figurative language to construct gender symbolically. For instance, I wrote that "we now see women in the *highest levels* of the most powerful professions." The phrase "highest levels" is an extremely common metaphor, what some call a "dead metaphor." By "dead" they mean a metaphor that is so common, so embedded in our language and worldviews, that we don't even notice it. Are professions like law and medicine literally "higher" than others? No. Yet, they are metaphorically. Attorneys and physicians tend to make more money, have more freedom, command greater prestige than, say, a first-grade teacher.

To begin to understand the ways in which humans figure gender, one can do no better than to turn back to Beauvoir. In the introduction to *The Second Sex*, she writes that

> first we must ask, what is a woman? 'Tota mulier in utero,' says one, 'woman is womb.' But in speaking of certain women, connoisseurs declare that they are not women, although they are equipped with a uterus like the rest. (p. xvi)

At stake here is a synecdoche disguised as a metaphor. Beauvoir has positioned one against the other two concepts of "woman," concepts that find their place in material reality. On one hand is the following metaphor: woman is womb. Is she literally? No. She is many things. Is womb metaphorically? According to some, yes. This metaphor depends on a synecdoche. One part of woman, literally, is the womb. Some would take this part of woman and use it to mark the whole: woman is womb.

On the other hand is a conflicting concept. These "connoisseurs" (written with at least a hint of irony, no doubt) recognize that the womb is part of the biological construction of the female, but refuse to be identified solely and only by this biological trait. In other words, they refuse the synecdochal identification, the worldview, that claims that woman is womb. Moreover, these connoisseurs refuse the label of woman, however er defined: apparently they fear being labeled only as womb. Despite the fact that literally they are women, they claim to be "not women": they refuse the literal for something else, a metaphorical state where they are neither men nor women.

The metaphorical claim that woman is womb is manifest in material reality in any number of ways. Consider, for instance, the adage that tells us that women should be barefoot, pregnant, and in the kitchen. They should be barefoot because their place is in the home, not outside. They should be pregnant because this is one of their primary functions: to birth babies. They should be in the kitchen because another primary function that they have, as mother and homeworker, is to cook for the family, to "mother" everybody.

How do women escape this figurative and material reduction of their lives? Some, as Beauvoir claims, escape by rejecting any identification as women. Others, and Beauvoir is one, accepts the symbolic and material "fact" that they are women. However, they attempt to redefine woman: woman has a womb, but is not a womb. Beauvoir writes that gender usually is constructed in the following ways (p. xxxi):

- Women are inferior to men
- Women are superior to men
- Women are equal to men

These options, not incidentally, often center around the Biblical story of the creation of humans in Genesis 2:4b and following. As Beauvoir notes, those who argue for the first—that women are inferior to men—point to this: Eve was created second, and she was created from Adam's rib. Eve is secondary and thus inferior. In this way, Eve is involved in a synecdochal relationship with Adam. She is part of the whole, but always an inferior part. She is a fragment, a piece.

Not so, proponents of the second option argue. Beauvoir tells us that these folk argue that Adam was the imperfect first draft. Only when God created Eve did God create the perfect human: Is she not smarter than Adam? More courageous? Here, God becomes a writer, a craftsperson, an engineer, an architect, one who works with "drafts." The writer, for instance, composes one draft only to revise. The second is the more polished, the more refined version.

Finally, proponents of the third option—that men and women are equal—argue that Adam and Eve were created as helpmates each to the other: they might have different functions, but they are complementary. Neither is superior to the other, neither inferior. These proponents resist the metaphorical positioning inherent in the words "inferior" and "superior." The word "inferior," after all, denotes a spatial position. If one is inferior, one is "below." If one is "superior," then, one is above.

All three camps depend, despite their differences, on analogical figuring. Here are the terms of the analogy:

Adam		Contemporary Men
————	as	————————
Eve		Contemporary Women

The debate centers not on the analogical scheme itself but on the subsidiary parts: What does the phrase "is to" mean? What does it mean to say "as"? Presumed is the power of the analogical connection: the story of Adam and Eve provides a model for how we can and should conceive and live out gender relationships in our own time. Supporting this analogy, and supported by it, is a worldview that states the following: Adam and Eve do matter, and thus, presumably, the Bible itself. People who conceive and live out gender relationships relative to the story of Adam and Eve in Genesis live within a world where the Bible matters.

Beauvoir herself rejects all three of these options. She writes that

> If we are to gain understanding, we must get out of these ruts; we must discard the vague notions of superiority, inferiority, equality which have hitherto corrupted every discussion of the subject and start afresh. (p. xxxi)

Beauvoir's metaphors could not be more powerful, more varied. None of the three options allow us to move forward or backward: we are stuck in their *ruts*: we can't travel any further down this path until we "get out of these ruts." To do so, we must *discard* the options. That is to say, we must see that these options are *garbage*, for what else do we discard but waste?

The entire volume of *The Second Sex* is Beauvoir's attempt to remove us from these ruts and put us on a new path. She wants to deposit the old options in waste bins and to conceive the issue anew. She wants to attend to the flashpoint of gender in a way that will counterpose the following problem. Woman is at once "a free and autonomous being like all human creatures" who "nevertheless finds herself living in a world where men compel her to assume the status of the Other" (p. xxxii). This is to say, man establishes his own position as superior to that of woman: woman is not really human in the way that men are. Seen through Beauvoir's eyes, central to gender is this fundamental problem, which is a problem of language at its root: Are women human like all other human creatures (which is to say, men) or are they not?

Working in a time and from a position in which women are not considered to be human like men are human, Beauvoir posits a simile: women, LIKE all other human creatures, are free and autonomous. The word "like" is crucial. At this moment in the text, Beavoir does not claim that women are human. If she did, her sentence might run something like this:

Woman, because she is human, is free and autonomous.

Such a sentence leaves no doubt: woman is human. Beauvoir's sentence, however, is another matter. Its use of the word "like" shows that Beauvoir well recognizes the ways in which the worldview of a sexist society supports, and is supported by, challenges, and is challenged by, figurative language. Woman is not seen as fully human. Rather, to paraphrase Beauvoir's words,

Woman, because she is woman, is OTHER than human. Thus, she is subject to male control.

Beauvoir, then, introduces the simile, which implies the following near-analogy: women have the same relationship to freedom and autonomy that all human creatures do. Read schematically, the near-analogy runs like this ("near" because it has three terms):

Woman		Human Creatures
———	as	———
Freedom and Autonomy		Freedom and Autonomy

For those of us who assume that woman is fully human, this analogical game seems almost absurd. Of course, we say, woman is human and thus is free and autonomous. Why play at this? Beauvoir, however, worked in a world where such an assumption could not be made easily.

Some would want to argue that even if one grants that Beauvoir's argument was important in its own time, it no longer has currency in our own. In the Western world, these folk would say, the worldview regarding women has changed dramatically. Women are freer, more autonomous, than ever they were before. Aren't more and more women physicians? Aren't more and more women business leaders? Aren't more and more women having fewer children at older ages?

Good questions, all. But, consider the still current practice of a bride taking her groom's family name when she marries. Here is a recent case in point. A young woman, a bright graduate student in a graduate program, a woman who wants a career, a family, a woman who certainly considers herself a free and autonomous human being, marries. Her professor, reading a set of student essays, notices a strange family name attached to a familiar first name. The professor realizes that the student has taken on her husband's name. Four questions rise in the professor's mind:

- Should I view this metaphorically?
- Should I view this ironically?
- Should I view this synecdochally?
- What does this say about my student's worldview relative to gender?

Viewed metaphorically, the name change indicates that the student now is what she literally isn't. In this way, the student has taken on a figure. She was born into one family, given a family name by at birth. She has now taken another, but what is it to take this other name? Is it any different than calling one thing by another name? Don't we all know that this is a figurative device? In this case, one can begin to argue that the student isn't as free and autonomous as she wants to think that she is. She has chosen to be named by her husband and his family, despite the fact that she has her own name. Apparently, she is not autonomous: her very identity now is defined not by her family, but by his.

Viewed ironically, the name change again indicates that the student, in fact, isn't as free and autonomous as she thinks she is. On one hand, one sees a woman who is bright, a woman who has a career, a woman who has family, friends, a woman who takes no grief from anyone in class. On the other, one sees a woman who now has taken on a subordinate role relative to her husband and husband's family. No longer is she identified by her given name, the name under which she constructed herself as an apparently free and autonomous human. Rather, she now is known only by her husband's name, marked, it seems, by him.

Viewed synecdochically, the picture is no less bleak. She is a part that is defined by another part, a part posing as the whole. If indeed marriage is the coming together of two parts to make a whole, when women take the men's family name, the men, at that moment, define the term of the marriage. It is as if number 1 married number 2 and instead of becoming number 3, they became number 2.

Consider as well the contemporary use of the slang term "hoe." "Hoe," spelled in its standard form, is the word "whore." Many contemporary song lyrics envision women as whores. These women are not literally prostitutes. Rather, all women are envisioned to be, finally and only, objects of sexual gratification. One small part of the phenomenon of women—prostitutes—has come to define the whole, metaphorically. Are all women whores? Of course not. Why do song composers and performers envision women in this way? It is not hard to guess, when one keeps Beauvoir in mind. Why do many people listen to these lyrics, without being offended? Again, it isn't hard to guess when one keeps Beauvoir in mind.

I could, of course, appeal to more studies and more books to make the case that gender is a flashpoint informed by figurative language. This move, however, simply would lead the persistent critic to wonder, again, if this isn't just the phantasm of books, which are, after all, symbolic constructs in and of themselves. I could also continue to point to my own lived reality and ask questions like these: Is it a marker of gender problems that women, on the whole, are the primary caregivers for their children? Is it a marker of gender problems that women continue to be raped? Is it a marker of gender problems that women continue to be beaten by their own husbands and boyfriends? Is it a marker of gender problems that many church bodies, including Roman Catholicism and the Southern Baptist Convention, refuse to ordain women, despite the fact that women comprise at least 50 percent of the most active members of these churches?

Rather than belabor this point, go on and on about my material reality and the ways in which we might begin to construct it symbolically, let me turn you to your own material reality, and ask you to figure it.

❖ *Exercise 4.1*

1. If your campus is in a neighborhood or near a business district, take a walk. Work street by street, watching in particular for men and women. Ask and answer questions like these: How are they dressed? What are they doing? How many of each do you see? Once you have gathered these notes together, organize what you have seen into categories. Then, ask yourself questions like these: What might these results say about the "gender dimensions" of the neighborhood in which my campus has its place? Have I used any figurative language in my notes, my answers? If so, what? What do they say about the worldview of the neighborhood? My own worldview?

2. Gather two or three unmarried female friends. Ask these questions of them: If you marry will you take your partner's name? Why? Then, gather two or three unmarried male friends. Ask these questions of them: If you marry, will you expect your partner to take your name? Why? Consider their answers. Have they used figurative language? If so, what? What worldviews do their answers reflect? Support? Challenge?

3. Interview an older woman, preferably one over the age of 50. Ask her to reflect on a) relationships between men and women in general; b) relationships between men and women in her own life. Ask her questions like these in particular: What changes have you seen? Are women and men at odds at times? Over what? If you could give one piece of advice about men to your great-granddaughter, what would it be? If you could give one piece of advice about women to your great-grandson, what would it be? Reflect on her responses, attending in particular to the figurative language that she used, to the worldview her responses reflect, support, challenge.

Whether you are an ardent feminist, a male chauvinist, or someone who is somewhere in between, you live in a world in which gender is a material reality that is constructed symbolically. Whether it is a "guy thing" or a "girl thing," a thing it is. It was no different for Sojourner Truth, who delivered a scathing speech about this flashpoint over one hundred years ago. It is to that speech that we now turn.

Sojourner Truth and "A'n't I a Woman?"

It is difficult for us in the twenty-first century to imagine the power and importance of public speaking in nineteenth century America. Full as we are with radio, television, film, and computers, we have no idea of what a world without mass media is. Imagine, if you can, a time when important public figures came to you only in one of three ways: through books, through newspaper accounts, or through a speech that you hear because you are part of the audience.

The nineteenth century was the great age of American public speaking: scholars shared their thoughts with large crowds at Chatauquas, preachers held forth in revival after revival, abolitionists and suffragettes held rallies across the United States. Indeed, the nineteenth century gave rise to perhaps the classical example of the American political debate, against which the debates of Gore v. Bush, Clinton v. Dole, Clinton v. Bush, Bush v. Dukakis, and so on seem anemic: Lincoln v. Douglass. The rally and the speech was the mass communication of the nineteenth century, and Sojourner Truth's "A'n't I a Woman?" is a one of the best of this media.

Truth, born a slave, was a worker not only for the emancipation of enslaved Americans, but also for the rights of women. Beauvoir argues that women are the Other subjugated by men, and this was certainly true in the nineteenth century. First and foremost, white men could enslave black American women. As slaves, these women were subject to the beck and call of their masters. White women, however, were oppressed Others, as well. Although not slaves, white women did not have the rights of citizenship accorded to white men. By the middle of the nineteenth century, this tension became a hot flashpoint, competing with the abolitionist movement for the nation's attention. It is at the center of this flashpoint that one can find Sojourner Truth and "A'n't I a Woman." You will find in Appendix C an account of the speech.

In a line from Mrs. Gage's account, one can see that indeed the women's movement was in competition with the Abolitionist movement. As Sojourner Truth rose to speak, a number of women in the audience reacted:

> Again and again, timorous and trembling ones came to me and said, with earnestness, "Don't let her speak, Mrs. Gage, it will ruin us. Every newspaper in the land will have our cause mixed up with aboli tion and niggers, and we shall be utterly denounced.

These women would have feared Sojourner Truth for two reasons. First, they might have wanted the group to focus on the matter at hand: the rights of women in a patriarchal society. To allow Sojourner Truth to speak was to chance a loss of focus: the group might start to think of the abolition of slavery rather than of the rights of women. Second, they might have been afraid of the abolitionist movement. It is one thing for mostly white women to claim their rights in a society dominated by white people. It is quite another for white women to advocate the abolition of slavery: after all, as white women they are still better off than African Americans, be they men or women.

The word "niggers" in this passage points to an irony, however unconsidered, however unintentional, that is central to this whole event. On one hand, a group of activist women are meeting to ask for fundamental change in the American social order. They see themselves as part of a synecdochal relationship, but men, on the whole, do not. The whole? America. The parts? Men and women. If indeed white women are part of the American whole, then, the activists claim, white women are an equal part.

On the other hand, at least some of these women do not want to think of black men and women in the same way. They themselves want to be emancipated, but they don't necessarily link their own emancipation with that of the slaves. This is particularly ironic when one considers the fact that many slaves, to say the least, were women.

Can they argue for emancipation of women without arguing, as well, for the abolition of slavery? If black women are slaves, they can't have the right to vote, for instance, until they are no longer slaves. To argue otherwise is to devour one's own argument: the irony is the snake that devours itself, tail first.

These women, however, might distinguish between white women and black women. They might say that when they argue for the emancipation of women, they argue for the emancipation of white women. Black female slaves are, they might say, another issue altogether. Perhaps. Perhaps they could say that when they, as white women, get the right to vote, they will help to free the slaves. Their stance, then, is strategic: it will be easier to secure equality for white women than it will be to free the slaves.

However, they still fall prey to racism. In their ironic, albeit strategic, fear of the abolitionist movement, they favor white women over black women. The irony is this: as feminists they align themselves not with all women, regardless of color, but with white men. It thus becomes, even if temporarily, white versus black. Gender then transforms into race, which raises a synecdochal issue. Of which whole are white women a part? Is their whole all women, or all white people?

Sojourner Truth was permitted to speak, however. She acknowledges the irony in the whispers, but challenges it:

> Wall, chilern, whar dar is so much racket dar must be somethin' out o' kilter. I tink dat 'twixt de niggers of de Souf and de womin at de Norf, all talkin' 'bout rights, de white men will be in a fix pretty soon.

Truth here aligns the abolitionist movement with the woman's movement: the Negroes of the south and the women of the north all talk about rights. The effect of all this talk is not division but unity: they present a combined front that the white man must confront.

Truth presumes a synecdochal relationship between the slaves, the white women of the north, and white men. All are parts of a whole. The white women can't ignore the slaves, nor the slaves the white women: they function as interlinked players. Neither can the white men ignore either the slaves or their women. Just as the slaves and the white women are linked to each other, the white men are linked to both.

The result of this synecdochal play is the "fix" in which white men will soon find themselves. "Fix" in this instance points to a predicament, a problem, a situation from which escape is unlikely. As a noun, "fix" reflects ironically its meaning as a verb, "to fix." As a verb, "to fix" demonstrates the ability to mend, to weave together, to make or repair a whole. In the terms of this book, "to fix" is to create or re-create the synecdochal relationship: the parts are brought together into the whole. As a noun, "fix" connotes a problem with the whole: it is breaking apart or broken. When one is in a fix, the problem needs to be fixed.

Analysis: "A'n't I a Woman?"

This section provides you the opportunity to engage in your own analytic study of Sojourner Truth's "A'n't I a Woman."

❖ *Exercise 4.2: Sentences*

Consider the following five sentences, all drawn from the text included in Appendix C. For each sentence, mark the tropes that are present. What kind are they? How do they work? Are they effective? As you answer these questions, attend to the worldviews that the tropes support and challenge.

1. One claimed superior rights and privileges for man, on the ground of "superior intellect"; another, because of the "manhood of Christ; if God had desired the equality of woman, He would have given some token of His will through the birth, life and death of the Saviour."

2. Dat man ober dar say dat womin needs to be helped into carriages, and lifted ober ditches, and to hab de best place everywhar.

3. I could work as much and eat as much as a man—when I could get it—and bear de lash as well!

4. If de fust woman God ever made was strong enough to turn de world upside down all alone, dese women togedder [and she glanced her eye over the platform] ought to be able to turn it back, and get it right side up again!

5. Amid roars of applause, she returned to her corner, leaving more than one of us with streaming eyes, and hearts beating with gratitude.

❖ *Exercise 4.3: Sections*

Consider three sections of the event as reported, quoted in the following list. For each section, mark the tropes that are present. What kind are they? How do they work? Are they effective? As you answer these questions, attend to the worldviews that the tropes support and challenge.

1. The second day, the work waxed warm. Methodist, Baptist, Episcopal, Presbyterian, and Universalist ministers came in to hear and discuss the resolutions presented.

2. And a'n't I a woman? Look at me! Look at my arm! [and she bared her right arm to the shoulder, showing her tremendous muscular power]. I have ploughed, and planted, and gathered into barns, and no man could head me! And a'n't I a woman?

3. "Den dat little man in black dar, he say women can't have as much rights as men, 'cause Christ wan't a woman! Whar did your Christ come from?" Rolling thunder couldn't have stilled that crowd, as did those deep, wonderful tones, as she stood there with outstretched arms and eyes of fire. Raising her voice still louder, she repeated, "Whar did your Christ come from? From God and a woman! Man had nothin' to do wid Him." Oh, what a rebuke that was to that little man.

❖ *Exercise 4.4: Topics*

Consider the following two tasks, both of which ask you to focus on the entire event included in Appendix C.

1. Consider the event as a whole. In a five-minute presentation to be delivered orally to your class, attend to the following questions: Which trope (metaphor or analogy or synecdoche or irony) is primary? This is to say, of all those used in the speech, which is the most central to the speech, the one without which the speech could not survive? What is the worldview that this trope supports? What is worldview that it challenges?

2. Consider the event as a whole. In a five-minute presentation to be delivered orally to your class, attend to the following questions: With

which trope (metaphor, analogy, synecdoche, or irony) would you describe the event? This should be your own trope, not one drawn from the text. Why this trope? What is the worldview that it supports? What is the worldview that it challenges? Does this trope indicate that you agree with Sojourner Truth? If so, why do you agree? Does it indicate that you disagree with Sojourner Truth? If so, why do you disagree?

❖ *Exercise 4.5: Figuring Gender*

The following exercises ask you to become public speakers on the topic of gender relationships. Each task requires you to take on a different guise, conduct different research. The point of each, however, is to require you to think of yourself as a member of a particular community that you want to move into a new understanding of the issue of gender in America. Use "A'n't I a Woman" as a model for your speeches in the following ways:

- Speak to your audience on occasion: use the second person singular pronoun, "you."

- Use questions and answers on occasion: try to create an atmosphere of dialogue.

- Draw on personal experience as well as texts to make your point.

- Don't hesitate to use "colloquial," "idiomatic," or even "slang," language.

1. Working with a group of three to four, choose a particular gender issue that strikes the group as very important. For instance, the group might decide that child-rearing is an important issue. Then, formulate this issue as a question. The group might ask a question like this: Should women continue as the primary caregivers for children? Each member of the group should prepare five-minute speeches on the issue, answering the question at hand. In order to develop the speech, work with many sources, but definitely a) conduct a survey of 10 people, gauging their responses to the issue. The survey should have five questions, each with a range of five possible responses, from "agree strongly" to "disagree strongly." Include for each item the option of "no opinion." Make reference to the results of this survey in your speech; b) draw on

your personal experience with this issue: use personal narrative in the text of your speech. Use no visual aids for this task.

2. Imagine that you have been asked to speak to a group of very powerful American men and women, comprising CEOs of corporations, clergy, politicians, military leaders, and the like. You have been asked, from the vantage point of your age and place, these two questions: what is the most pressing problem between men and women today and what can we do to fix it? In a five-minute speech, answer these questions. Draw on a variety of sources, but definitely draw on three: a) a speech on gender relationships (other than "A'n't I a Woman") that you discover through library or Internet research; b) the Bible; c) either the Declaration of Independence or the Constitution of the United States of America. Use one visual aid for this speech. Keep in mind that you are speaking to a group of 50. Use the visual aid in a way that all can see it. Do not use a visual aid that you read, such as a portion of your speech. Use the visual aid as an aid: a text (be it a picture, a diagram, etc.) to help you make your point.

5

Figuring the Environment

The Environment as Symbolic Construct and Material Reality

In his germinal essay, "What Hath Man Wrought?" (*America* 1967), Lynn T. White, Jr., holds that "all forms of life modify their contexts" (p. 11). He is speaking here not of linguistic contexts, not of epistemic contexts, but of social contexts, and social contexts of a particular sort: what humans call "nature." Life, he rightly presumes, is impossible otherwise. The very act of inhalation and exhalation is an act of modification: the creature takes the oxygen that was in the air and replaces it with carbon dioxide. Is this act of modification good? No. Is it bad? No. It simply is the way it is. Creatures who survive in part by inhaling and processing oxygen and by expelling the waste product—carbon dioxide—are acting neither ethically nor unethically, neither morally nor immorally when they breathe. They simply function as they are meant to function.

The word "modify," then, can have this sense: it is a matter of being. So, too, modify can be understood to denote a good action, an action that is more than simply a matter of being. Consider, for instance, what White has to say about the humble "coral polyp": "By serving its own ends, it has created a vast undersea world favorable to thousands of other kinds of animals and plants" (p. 11). As the polyp flourishes, it modifies its contexts in such a way that many, many other species are able to flourish. If "flourishing" is understood to be a hallmark of the good, then, indeed, the coral polyp's modification of its context is more than being: it is a good action.

Writing as he does in late 1967, at the beginning of what can be called a time of ecological awareness, White also knows that modifications of the natural context in which one lives can be understood as negative. Indeed, it is one thing simply to breathe. It is another thing to modify one's context in such a way that one, and others, are able to flourish. It is yet another thing to modify one's context in such a way that one calls into question not only the ability of others' to flourish, but, indeed, one's own ability to flourish.

This is particularly problematic, White notes, when the modification is undertaken by a species as numerous, and as scientifically and technologically advanced, as humans. Human modification of the natural context in which humans find life has led us deep into what White calls an "ecologic crisis" (p. 49). He writes that

> With the population explosion, the carcinoma of planless urban-ism, the now geological deposits of sewage and garbage, surely no creature other than man has ever managed to foul its nest in such short order. (p. 13)

This sentence deserves further consideration because it makes one aware of the fine line between the metaphor and the literal, the scientific use of literal language and the imaginative use of figurative. Consider these two phrases:

- Carcinoma of planless urbanism
- Geological deposits of sewage and garbage

The metaphor of the first phrase is obvious, powerful. The movement of human populations into cities—the phenomenon of urbanization—is called a "cancer" because it is planless. Cities sprawl, White implies, killing surrounding countryside. Thus, the metaphor implies an analogy:

$$\frac{\text{Cancer Cells}}{\text{Human Body}} \quad \text{as} \quad \frac{\text{Planless Urbanism}}{\text{Earth}}$$

The second phrase, likewise, is metaphoric. Normally, the word "geologic" connotes earth and rock: those layers studied by geologists in order to understand certain properties of the earth. When one walks into a geology class, for instance, one expects to study such things as rock formations, layers of rock and dirt underneath the soil upon which we walk, the shifting of rock plates, and volcanic activity. One does not, normally, expect to study sewage and garbage. Sewage and garbage, normally understood, are not geologic in nature.

However, White suggests that the human modification of the natural context invites a metaphor. Consider, for instance, the dump of the small New Hampshire town in which I live. Every other week or so I load the back end of my Subaru with the garbage from our house. We dutifully recycle and compost, being children of the era in which there is an ecologic crisis. That said, the amount of trash I take to the dump every two weeks is not insubstantial. Once at the landfill, I back my Subaru to the edge of the dump and park. I then proceed to toss my bags of garbage—anything not compostable or recyclable—into the dump. As I do so, many others act likewise, just as many others have done before us, just as many others will do after us. All the while, an enormous front-end loader travels back and forth across the garbage, crushing it into the ground. It then covers this layer with dirt, more people throw garbage onto the dirt, the garbage is crushed into the ground and so on, layer after layer after layer. Although I have not lived in my town for long, many people have told me that they have watched a mountain grow over the years. It is, of course, a mountain of garbage.

Does this mean that it is not a real mountain? Normally, of course, one does not think of a "real" mountain as a geologic feature formed by garbage. However, and this is the point of White's phrase, we have created mountains of garbage and sewage. Multitudinous sedimentary layers of human waste have modified, and continue to modify, the context in which we live. Is this modification necessary? Yes. After all, humans create waste and must dispose of it. Is it good? In a way. After all, the localization and isolation of human waste is better than, say, simply dumping it out of our doors and windows into our streets and yards. Is it bad? Without a doubt, given the size and scope both of the human population and the waste that this population generates. My town's dump is scheduled to go out of operation in the next year or two: it will soon run out of space; the mountain will have grown to its full height. Where does the garbage go then? We will dump it into a waiting trailer, to be hauled to other towns that still have mountains to build. When those towns have built their mountains, the geologic becomes, perhaps, catastrophic.

Humans not only figure the tension between themselves and the environment. They also conflict with each other as to how to deal with the conflict between themselves and nature, and they figure this tension as well. As White notes, we have not agreed on what this attention might be: "What shall we do? No one yet knows" (p. 13). He maintains that there have been many ideas put forth, at least as of 1967, but all are problematic. Most simplistic are those that call for "prettification": tear down billboards, plant wildflowers along the edges of, and in the medians between, highways, and the like. Most extreme are those that advocate "deep-freezing" particular ecosystems: return the High Sierra to the state it was in before "the first Kleenex was dropped" (p. 13).

In their article "Marx Meets Muir: Toward a Synthesis of the Progressive Political and Ecological Visions" (*Tikkun* 2.4) Frances Moore Lappè and J. Baird Callicott note that even among so-called "progressives" there is conflict. Many political activists and theorists who are concerned about three other flashpoints around which this book centers—namely, race and class—think that "environmental amenities—pure air and water, landscaped green belts, plenty of park land and wilderness—are luxury items for well-heeled yuppies" (p. 16).

This quotation, it needs to be said, is informed at its core by figurative language. The irony of the word "amenities" is powerful: Is clean air and water an amenity or a necessity for human life? So, too, the phrase "well-heeled" is a metaphor that emerges from and is supported by class conflict. It is rooted in a time when people went to cobblers to have their shoes resoled rather than simply throwing them out when they showed wear. Those who are well-heeled are those who have money to resole their shoes. Those who are not well-heeled have not enough money even to "put clothes on their back."

In conflict with this group of political activists and theorists, according to Lappè and Moore, are "the environmentalists and deep ecologists" (p. 16). They claim that the political "progressives lack biological diversity: They see nature not as a living, functioning system, but as an inexhaustible emporium and as a mere stage upon which political struggles are acted out" (p. 16). Again, figurative language is powerfully present. The very term "deep ecologists" is metaphoric. It connotes a group of people who somehow are closer to the crisis, closer to earth, the air, the water. They are "deep," as opposed to those who are shallow. Then, too, they claim that the so-called progressives treat nature not literally as a living being but, rather, metaphorically: it is a store (hence emporium) of goods to be consumed. It is a place where they create dramas: all of which are not real, but simply acts.

Lappè and Moore point here to a conflict in worldviews, a conflict revealed in the figurative language. The political progressives' worldview privileges the poor, the oppressed racial minorities, and women. They link concerns about nature to the elite classes who oppress the poor, to the elite racial groups who oppress the racial minorities. Conversely, the deep ecologists' worldview privileges nature itself. Those who do privilege nature are, first and foremost, shallow ecologists if ecologists at all. Second, these political progressives treat nature as a tool, an instrument, a thing, an object.

Lappè and Moore, on one hand, and White, on the other, seek different ways to address this flashpoint. Lappè and Moore turn to Karl Marx and John Muir—political progressive and deep ecologist; White, as we shall see, turns to St. Francis. However, all agree that a change in worldview is in order. Lappè and Moore seek to unite and transform two camps that are at odds with each other. White seeks to reinvent the Western worldview itself.

White argues that we need a change in consciousness, a change in the very worldview that has supported the ecologic crisis in the first place. For those of us in the Occident, this is the worldview supported by, defined by, articulated by, Christianity (pp. 17–18). White writes that "more science and more technology are not going to get us out of the present ecologic crisis until we find a new religion, or rethink our old one" (p. 18). He rejects the former for numerous reasons. He chooses, rather, to rethink the worldview supported by Christianity and turn to St. Francis. First, White argues, we must "reject the Christian axiom that nature has no reason for existence save to serve man" (p. 18). Second, he proposes that we should adopt St. Francis as the "patron saint for ecologists" (p. 18). He claims that St. Francis "tried to substitute the idea of equality of all creatures, including man, for the idea of man's limitless rule of all creation" (p. 18). White's ideas are significant here because again he demonstrates how it is that within flashpoints in general, and this flashpoint in particular, worldview and figurative language work together.

Consider, for instance, the phrase "patron saint for ecologists." Undoubtedly, this is a metaphor. It may be the case that some ecologists are Roman Catholic, and that some of these Roman Catholic ecologists, in the privacy of their own hearts, think of St. Francis as the patron saint of their professional work. For those ecologists—many that they probably are—who are neither Roman Catholic nor even theistic, White's claim is shocking. Saints, at least within the Christian world, are, for the most part, part of worldviews of Roman Catholics, not Protestants. In fact, a host of Protestants—Southern Baptists, Presbyterians, Methodists—find the Roman Catholic appeal to saints odd at best, heretical at worst. Moreover, saints are part of the worldview of theists, those people who believe in God. Atheists and agnostics have no reason to look to patron saints because saints, by definition, are mediators between humans and God.

White, certainly, does not wish to convert non-Roman Catholics to Catholicism, atheists and agnostics to theism. Rather, White invokes a metaphor here to make a point about worldview. He argues that science and technology alone cannot solve the ecological crisis. Rather, he claims, humans in the West must change their worldviews. He offers St. Francis as the mark, as the model, of this change. No longer will we view the world as our private domain, much the same as King Leopold of Belgium saw the Congo as his. Rather, St. Francis, as marker and model, will reorient us: we will see ourselves as equal to other creatures, other forms of life.

Implied in this metaphor, as is the case with many metaphors, is an analogy:

$$\frac{\text{Saints}}{\text{Roman Catholics}} \quad \text{as} \quad \frac{\text{St. Francis}}{\text{Ecologists}}$$

White suggests that ecologists should take on St. Francis as if they are devoted Roman Catholics. Just as saints provide Roman Catholics with guidance, with mediation, with hope, with the marked presence of the divine will, so, too, St. Francis will provide ecologists—indeed all of us, by implication—with a new orientation. No longer will we view the world as an emporium for human consumption.

Or, as White writes it, we will come "to substitute the idea of equality of all creatures, including man, for the idea of man's limitless rule of all creation." That is to say, humans will reinvent their worldviews so that they no longer see themselves as "rulers." This word—implied analogy that it is—is important because it indicates a worldview that must be overcome, according to White. The implied analogy is this:

$$\frac{\text{King}}{\text{Subjects}} \quad \text{as} \quad \frac{\text{Humans}}{\text{Nature}}$$

Thus, humans relate to nature as a King relates to his subjects. At its best, this world is benevolent: the king protects his subjects and the subjects love the king. This, to be sure, is the world mythologized by the Arthurian legends. King Arthur vanquishes his foes; he creates Camelot, a kingdom of virtue, peace, tranquility.

Rarely, of course, is the world so benevolent. At its worst, the world of the monarchy includes kings, and queens, who view their subjects as vassals: servants who owe the monarchy loyalty, service, goods, and money. The vassals, for their part, are subjugated, suffering, full of torment, rage, and rebellion. White would have us forgo this worldview and move toward a democracy of sorts: we would view ourselves—following St. Francis—as siblings of the created order. St. Francis's great hymn records this view: brother sun and sister moon.

This struggle between worldviews—human as ruler of the created order and human as sibling to it—is recorded in one of the great narratives of the West: the story of the creation of the Earth as recorded in the first three chapters of the book of Genesis. Biblical scholars have long argued that these three chapters include not one but two creation stories. The first is contained in Genesis 1-2:4a. It provides a narrative well-known even to the most devout of atheists. Out of nothing God created light and darkness, birds of the air, fishes of the sea, animals of the land.

Only on the sixth day did God create humans and then, in an act of kingly trust, granted humans "dominion" over all creation. It is true that much discussion over the term "dominion" has taken place. Does it mean, for instance, that humans may wantonly treat the created order as they will, like bad kings? Or, does it mean that, like King Arthur, they are responsible for Camelot, for a Kingdom devoted to a chivalrous code of conduct? In either case, one connotation of the word seems clear. Humans exist above the order: they were created last and given control over it.

In contrast stands the second creation story, Genesis 2:4b and following. This story is likewise very familiar, even to the most devout of atheists. Here Adam is created first. He is lonely, God notes, and so brings other animals to him. Adam proceeds to name them, but none prove companionable, in the fullest sense of that term. So, God creates Eve. Until those fateful bites, Adam and Even live naked in the Garden. It is a place without toil, without bloodshed, without strife. Even God walks amidst the Garden, apparently, for how else could God have missed Adam and Eve? In this story, humans have not been given dominion over the created order. Rather, they are siblings to it. Consider that God intially thought that the animals might make fit companions for Adam. This is understandable because Adam and animals alike are created from the ground (2:7; 2:18–20). Thus, Adam and the animals have a synecdochal relationship. Both are parts of the same whole:

Adam—Ground—Animals

This synecdoche marks a worldview in which Adam and the animals are kin. The connection between Adam and the animals continues even after Adam rejects them as companions. Although they do not meet Adam's ultimate needs and desires, neither are they hated nor despised. Apparently, they continue to live in the Garden with Adam and Eve until the Fall.

This conflict—between an analogy of dominion on one hand and a synecdoche of siblinghood on the other—continues in contemporary America. Consider the following:

- A logging company marks an old-growth forest in the Pacific Northwest for cutting. Included are ancient redwoods, some which predate the movement of the Europeans into America.

The company wants to cut the forest in order to supply home-builders and furnituremakers around the world with wood so that they can serve burgeoning human populations. In order to stop the logging, a young activist with the environmental group EarthFirst! makes a decision. She climbs one of the trees and lives on a platform until the logging company guarantees that it will save some of the trees.

- In 1999, an environmental activist reads about the problem of overfishing in the Gulf of Maine and the Georges Bank off the coast of New England. She also reads that as a result, the Federal Government drastically restricts the length of the commercial fishing season and the size of the catches that fishermen are allowed to haul in. The activist notices that both the fishing industry and the Federal Government refer to fish as "stock," as in, "there has been a monumental decline in the cod stock." The fishermen wait for the day when the stock has been rebuilt so that they can fish again. Reflecting on the word "stock," the environmental activist wonders if these people—fishermen and government officials alike—view the ocean as a store constructed for human customers. The cod in the ocean are, it seems, already like bags of frozen fish on the grocery shelves: the stock is low, and it needs to be replenished.

Rather than belabor these reflections, I turn you to yourselves. The following exercise will help you discover in your own lives the ways in which humans figure the environment.

❖ *Exercise 5.1*

1. Consider the word "nature." We use it all the time, but probably would not be able to provide quickly a concise definition. Using the Oxford English Dictionary, study definitions of the word "nature" as it refers to the environment. Are these definitions negative or positive? Then, ask yourself these two questions: Are any of these tropes? What is the worldview revealed by these tropes?

2. Find one friend or acquaintance who is a vegetarian and another who eats meat. Separately or together, interview them. Ask the following questions and others that you might compose: Why do vegetarians not eat meat? Why do meat eaters eat meat? To the vegetarian:

Would you be willing to eat meat if you had to in order to survive? If not, why? If so, why? To the meat eater: have you ever killed the animal that you eat? Describe it. If not, would you be willing to kill an animal in order to eat it? Why? Study their language: Are they using tropes? What worldviews do their answers reveal?

Whether you are a vegetarian or an meat eater, a nature lover or city lover, one who thinks that humans have dominion over the remainder of creation or one who sides with St. Francis, you live in a world marked by division, conflict, and confusion over the relationship of humans to "nature." It is in this world that Gary Snyder composed his poem, "For All." Both this poem and his "Breasts" are included in Appendix D.

Gary Snyder and "For All"

As a poet and intellectual, Snyder has been a major force in the American countercultural movement. An original member of the so-called "Beat Generation" of writers, Snyder has been at the center of the environmental movement since its inception in the late 1960s. In addition, Snyder has been deeply influenced by Native American mythology as well as Zen Buddhism. He stands firmly against Western industrial and technological understanding of what it is to be human. Humans, according to Snyder, do not have dominion over the Earth. Rather, humans are part of it and must find their place within it. Nowhere is this more apparent than in "For All," published as part of the collection titled *Axe Handles* (1983).

The dedication of *Axe Handles* itself orients the reader within Snyder's world. Most books are dedicated to spouses, children, friends, parents, lovers. In contrast, *Axe Handles* is dedicated to a geographic location: "This book is for San Juan Ridge." Snyder proclaims that he has written this book not for a spouse, not for a child, not for a friend, not for a parent, not for a lover, but for a mountain range. Is this a metaphor? No. Snyder literally dedicates his book to rocks, earth, trees, and the animals that therein dwell. Is it ironic? No. Snyder does not look for us to find an opposing meaning. It is as it is: a dedication to a place. It is, thus, synecdochal, at least by implication. With this dedication, Snyder declares himself to be part of the whole of the natural order, focusing in particular on the San Juan Ridge. Most dedications are, indeed, synecdochal. They provide the author of book the opportunity to claim citizenship within a larger circle: be it that of friends, family, even colleagues. Snyder, in contrast, locates himself as part of the larger natural order: he claims kinship with the San Juan Ridge.

So, too, in "For All" Snyder locates himself synecdochally not within a larger frame of human relationships but with a larger frame of relationship with the natural world. This begins in the first stanza, where he celebrates the moment of fording a river:

> Ah to be alive
> on a mid-September morn
> fording a stream
> barefoot, pants rolled up,
> holding boots, pack on,
> sunshine, ice in the shallows,
> northern rockies.

Here Snyder uses the language of simple description, much like a scientific naturalist. Rather than shifting into metaphorical fancy by which he might declare the stream to be "liquid heaven," or some such figure, he describes the event as he experiences it. He tells us what he is doing (fording), when he is doing it (mid-September), how he is doing it (with a feeling of joy, pants rolled up, pack on, holding boots), and where he is doing it (in the northern Rockies).

The naturalistic description continues into the second stanza, but then shifts abruptly with the simple phrase, "I pledge allegiance." With this phrase, Snyder finds himself in strange company: he travels now with the American Roman Catholic Bishops in their pastoral letter, *Economic Justice for All.* As we saw in Chapter 3, the Bishops invoke parts of "The Pledge of Allegiance" in order to make their case for a reordering of the American economy. So too Snyder begins to invoke "The Pledge of Allegiance" in order to make his case for a reordering of humanity's relationship to the natural order.

I say that Snyder finds himself in strange company because he is decidedly not Roman Catholic, nor even Christian. Snyder is a practicing Zen Buddhist with deep affiliation to certain Native American mythic practices. On one hand, it is strange for him to be traveling with the

Bishops. On the other hand, it isn't strange at all. The fact that both Snyder and the Bishops use "The Pledge of Allegiance" points to the synecdochal character of citizenship. What do I mean by the "synecdochal character of citizenship?" This: all Americans are part of a whole, which is the language of the country. Despite the fact that Snyder and the Bishops are fundamentally different in terms of religious practice, they are part of the same fabric of language. "The Pledge of Allegiance" is part of Snyder and the Bishops, just as they are part of the culture that teaches it to its young.

However, Snyder and the Bishops use the "The Pledge of Allegiance" very differently. The Bishops use it to recast economic relationships, whereas Snyder uses it ironically to establish a new synecdochal relationship with the natural order. Consider, for instance, these lines:

> I pledge allegiance to the soil
> of Turtle Island,

The implied analogy of these lines is as follows:

Americans		Snyder
———	as	———
America		Turtle Island

Ritually, one act that binds Americans to their country is the "The Pledge of Allegiance": they plege loyalty both to the flag and to "the republic for which it stands." Snyder counterposes himself to the typical American: he pledges allegiance not to a flag and the flag's corresponding country, but to the earth itself.

Therein lies the new synecdochal relationship. Just as the dedication to *Axe Handles* indicates a reorientation, "For All" does so, as well. Snyder might see himself as part of the larger whole, which is the American republic (indeed, he has written poems that show that he does). In "For All," however, his primary relationship is not with a nation but with the earth upon which the nation has constructed itself. He is part of the stream through which he walks. He is part of the Rockies through which the stream flows. He is part of the sun that shines upon the Rockies through which the stream flows.

This, then, is where the irony begins to emerge. It is ironic that Snyder uses the language of political ritual to bind himself to an apolitical entity: the earth itself. Indeed, America as a nation is culpable for the environmental destruction that Snyder decries often in his poetry. As you can read in "Breasts," Snyder mourns the poisonous presence of "deadly molecules hooked up in strings". Surely American industry, part of, and supported by, the American republic, has introduced deadly molecules into the natural order. One might expect Snyder to reject the ritualistic political language of America in order to embrace the earth. Instead, ironically, he finds within this language the hope of reordering. Rather than pledge himself to a political entity that often hurts the earth, he uses that political entity's language to declare himself part of that which the political entity hurts.

At this point, a deeper irony emerges: Snyder pledges himself to "Turtle Island." "Turtle Island" is the name for North America used by some Native peoples on the West Coast of this country. Under the name "America" is another name, a name used by peoples decimated by the European onslaught. With the term "Turtle Island," Snyder heightens the ironic tension. Here is the scheme:

1. The American republic was established by Europeans who marched across the country, decimating the native peoples.

2. Americans pledge allegiance to the flag and to the republic for which it stands.

3. Snyder uses this pledge to remember the name for this land once used by peoples who were decimated by the Europeans who established the republic and the pledge itself.

In essence, Snyder uses the ritual political language of the conquering people to challenge the conquering people themselves. He pledges allegiance to that which they thought they had conquered.

Analysis: "For All" and "Breasts"

This section provides you the opportunity to engage in your own analytic study of Snyder's poetry included in Appendix D.

❖ *Exercise 5.2: Words*

Consider the following five words and phrases, all drawn from the texts included in Appendix D. For each word, consider these questions: Is it a trope? Does it imply a trope? What kind? How does it work? Is it effective? As you answer these questions, attend to the worldviews that the words support and challenge.

1. "creek music" ("For All")

2. "heart music" ("For All")

3. "interpenetration" ("For All")

4. "But the breast is a filter" ("Breasts")

5. "we celebrate breasts" ("Breasts")

❖ *Exercise 5.3: Sections*

Consider parts of the poems, quoted in the following list. All are drawn from the texts included in Appendix D. For each section, mark the tropes that are present. What kind are they? How do they work? Are they effective? As you answer these questions, attend to the worldviews that the tropes support and challenge.

1. From "For All":
   I pledge allegiance to the soil
           of Turtle Island,
   and to the beings who thereon dwell

2. From "For All":
   One ecosystem
   In diversity
           Under the sun
   With joyful interpenetration for all.

3. From "Breasts":
   So we celebrate breasts
   We all love to kiss them
           —they're like philosophers!
   Who hold back the bitter in mind

To let the more tasty
Wisdom slip through
    for the little ones.
    who can't take the poison so young.

❖ Exercise 5.4: Topics

Consider the following two tasks, both of which ask you to focus on the poems included in Appendix D.

1. Consider "Breasts" or "For All." In a 3-4 page essay written for your class, attend to the following questions: Which trope is primary? This is to say, of all those used in the poem, which is the most central to the text, the one without which the text could not survive? What is the worldview that this trope supports? What is worldview that it challenges?

2. Consider "Breasts" or "For All". In a 3–4 page essay written to be read by Snyder, attend to the following questions: With which trope would you describe the poem? This should be your own, not one drawn from the text. Why this trope? What is the worldview that it supports? What is the worldview that it challenges? Does this trope indicate that you disagree with Snyder? If so, why do you disagree? Does it indicate that you agree with Snyder? If so, why do you agree?

❖ Exercise 5.5: Figuring the Environment

The following exercise asks you yourself to become a poet on the topic of the environment. As you are working on these tasks, remember that there are many ways to write wonderful poetry. This is simply one way to go about it, using Snyder's poems as models for your own. Use his poems as models in the following ways:

- Do not use end rhymes.
- Feel free to start lines away from the left edge of the page. Start the lines where they should be: attend to the sound of the poem, the movement of the images and the ideas.

- Fill your poems with very concrete, particular descriptions of the thing and place.

- Use these descriptions as a way to reflect abstractly on the ways in which humans do, or should, interact with the environment.

- Attend consciously to the use of tropes in your poetry, especially metaphor, analogy, irony, and synecdoche.

1. Compose a poem that has at least 20 lines and three to four stanzas. Each of the stanzas should represent a shift in topic, idea, description, or focus. The subject of the poem should be a place in the natural world that you find either particularly beautiful or particularly ugly. In the poem, describe and/or comment on the place.

2. Compose a poem that has at least 20 lines and three to four stanzas. Each of the stanzas should represent a shift in topic, idea, description, or focus. The subject of the poem should be an organic creature or part of an organic creature, for example, a cow or the horns of a cow, a bird or the wings of a bird. In the poem, describe and/or comment on the creature or part of the creature.

6

Figuring War

War as Symbolic Construct and Material Reality

To say that war is a flashpoint is, perhaps, redundant. Of the five topics of concern in this book—race, class, gender, the environment, and war—war is closest to the literal meaning of the term "flashpoint." War, after all, involves flames of various kinds: the tiny burst that ignites the bullet's travel from shell casing to body; the explosion of the tank "killed" by a U.S. Marine Warthog aircraft; the flaming city, recently attacked by high-altitude bombers.

Of course, this book is not about the thing itself, but about discourse, and the figures we use in discourse to talk about the thing. It is not about race, but about ways in which we figure race. It is not about class but about ways in which we figure class. It is not about gender, but about ways in which we figure gender. It is not about the environment, but about ways in which we figure the environment. So, too, with war. This chapter deals not with the theory of war, the strategy of war, the reality of war, but with ways in which we "figure" war: how we use metaphor, analogy, synecdoche, and irony to frame, to explore, to villify, and to glorify war. Consider, for instance, the *Iliad* and its great hero, Odysseus. Paris of Troy, as we know, stole Helen away from the great Spartan king Menelaus with the blessing of Aphrodite, the goddess of love.

As the most beautiful woman in the world, Helen was courted by many. In order to forestall the shedding of blood over her, Odysseus concocted a plan. Whoever won Helen's hand would be free to marry her. All other suitors would pledge to come to Helen's aid should she need it. The suitors agreed. Menelaus won her hand, and Odysseus himself married Penelope, Helen's cousin. When Paris took Helen away to Troy, Menelaus called on the suitors to win her back. Odysseus tried to hide from this fate, sensing the oncoming tragedy, not wanting to leave his wife, his son, and his beloved Ithaca. He was found and was forced to honor his scheme. For 10 years, the *Iliad* tells us, battle raged outside the great walled city of Troy. Was it glorious? Yes. Many heroes proved themselves over and over again. Was it tragic and senseless? Yes. Many heroes, not to mention the citizens of Troy, lost their lives over the hand of a single woman. Odysseus could not wait to extricate himself and his warriors from this affair. When he did, he left only to spend the next 10 years wandering on an odyssey. For Odysseus, at least, the Trojan War brought only 20 years of separation from his wife, his son, his beloved Ithaca, brought only the death of all of his warriors save himself.

Consider, as well, the Christian Bible. One figure central to the Christian worldview is King David, not only as psalmist, but as warrior as well. After all, it was David who, as a boy, did what the Israelite army could not. While they cowered in fear of Goliath, David marched boldly out to meet the giant and defeat him, armed only with a sling, some stones, and faith in God. In opposition to David stands Jesus, the central figure in the Christian drama. Jesus, the Gospels tell us, chastised one of his followers in the Garden of Gethsemane when this follower sliced off the Roman soldier's ear. It was a moment when a battle, perhaps, could have begun. Jesus had just completed a triumphant week in Jerusalem, and his closest followers, apparently, were armed. Rather than promote war, however, Jesus told his follower that war was not the path to be followed. The follower sheathed his sword, Jesus healed the Roman soldier's ear, and the rest, as they say, is history.

Important to remember about the Jesus story is this: he is considered to be a descendant of King David, from the root of Jesse. Indeed, the Gospel of Matthew opens with a geneaology that traces Jesus back to

David. Central to the Christian drama is this tension: Jesus, who denies the validity of war, is the heir of Israel's greatest king. One might suggest, certainly, Jesus and David are not in conflict. Rather, Jesus has replaced David. Pacifism has replaced militarism. This is true, to be sure, for Christian pacifists. It is not true, however, for Christians who participate in war. They might not like it, but they see it as a necessary part of human life. Do Christians glorify war and warriors? Absolutely. Do they villify it and wish it didn't have to be? Absolutely. Therein lies the discursive tension. People's worldviews about war are in conflict.

Central to the Greek stories about the Trojan War and to the Biblical stories about David and Jesus are tropes. Central, as well, to our own world are tropes that arise from these foundational stories about war. Odysseus, for instance, is said to be as clever as a fox. The analogy is this:

Odysseus		Fox
————	as	——
Political Decisions		Survival Decisions

That is to say, just as fox is clever enough to survive in the wild, Odysseus is clever enough to survive in the tangle of Grecian politics.

Consider, as well, a figure central to the *Iliad*: Achilles, perhaps the greatest Greek warrior. He was killed by an arrow during the Trojan War, shot from Paris's bow, guided by the Gods. Where was he shot? His heel, of course, the one place not dipped in the fire of immortality by his mother, a minor goddess. Physiologically, we all share that same spot. Metaphorically we have it as well. One might hear, for instance, this question: "What is his Achilles' heel?" This metaphor means, "What is his weakness?" The larger metaphorical scheme into which this fits is one of war. The one who asks the question wonders how it is that the person can be killed, at least metaphorically, where it is that a deadly arrow can penetrate.

So, too, the stories of David the warrior and Jesus the peacemaker are rife with tropes. Goliath, seeing the approach of David, says, "Am I a dog for you to come against me with sticks?" The giant Philistine is outraged to see that the Israelites have sent against him a boy, a boy not even clothed in the armor of war. He invokes this analogy, hidden in the question:

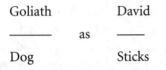

Goliath, not surprisingly, is insulted. He takes the approach of David as a metaphorical insult: he has been called a dog, or so he thinks. He interprets the approach of David as belittling, as if the Israelites did not fear him, respect him. In turn, he insults David: the lad is not even a lad, but sticks sent to beat the dog.

How often in our own time do we hear the metaphor of David and Goliath invoked? It is not uncommon for us to speak of a seemingly smaller and weaker opponent facing a larger and stronger adversary and speak of "David and Goliath." The larger implication is that this event will be like the Biblical story: the small will crush the large.

One Christian group that has steadfastly interpreted Jesus as a pacifist, and interpreted the Bible as preferring the way of peace to the way of war, is the Quaker. Along with the Mennonites and Brethren, Quakers consistently have declared that war is an affront to humankind, that to prepare for war, to celebrate war, is a grave error, counter to the way in which humans are meant to live. Quaker declarations, not surprisingly, are shaped by figurative language.

Consider, for instance, the "Eleventh Query" published by the Ohio Valley Yearly Meeting of the Religious Society of Friends in its *Book of Discipline* (1978). It reads

> Do you live in the life and power which takes away the occasion for all wars? Do you, on Christian principles, refuse to participate in or cooperate with all military effort? Do you work actively for peace and the removal of the causes of wars? Do you endeavor to cultivate good will, mutual understanding and equal opportunities for all races, creeds, and nations? Have you examined your life style and possessions to make sure that the seeds of war are not found within them? (p. 67)

Queries are questions used by Quakers as points of discernment: they guide Quakers in their worship and in their life practice. As such, they are meant to become part of the architecture of the Quaker worldview. As the "Eleventh Query" makes clear, these questions are meant to permeate life outside the Quaker meetinghouse: the Quaker theology and sociopolitical views interpenetrate each other.

Thus, Quakers within the Ohio Valley Yearly Meeting are asked this in the very first sentence: "Do you live in the life and power which takes away the occasion for all wars?" This one sentence is charged with both metaphor and synecdoche. The metaphor is as follows:

Life and Power = God

This is an implied metaphor, understandable as such when one consid ers the second sentence of the Query. Quakers clearly identify themselves as a Christian body. Once this is established, it is easy to understand that the life and power of the Christian worldview is God.

Is God literally "life and power?" No. God literally is not anything identifiable in human terms, at least for Jews and Christians. Any attempt, in fact, to so identify God is to commit idolatry. The story of Moses and the people of Israel escaping from Egypt is testament to this. God appears as a burning bush, a column of fire: God is both and neither. When Moses, kneeling before the burning bush asks God to identify Godself, God replies, "I will be who I will be" (YHWH).

The synecdoche embedded in the first sentence of the Query centers around the same phrase, "life and power." To ask whether or not one lives "in" the life and power is to ask whether or not one is part of a greater whole. The burden of the synecdoche rests on the preposition, "in." The Query doesn't ask if one lives next to it, on it, underneath it, or on top of it. Rather, it uses a preposition that claims a synecdochal relationship, a relationship of part to whole. If a person is "in" something, that person is part of that something. Moreover, that something is necessarily larger: it must be so in order to accommodate the person. For instance, one might ask, "Are you *in* the group, or out?" This is to say, are you part of the larger whole, which is the group?

The larger whole, in the case of the Query, is the life and the power, or, God. The Query asks of the Quaker, then, this: Are you part of God or not? If you are, the question implies that you will live within a whole of which war is not a part. The life and the power, so the first question tells us, "takes away the occasion for all wars."

Deeper in the Query one finds competing gardening metaphors, suggesting that the human is both a cultivator and a thing to be cultivated. In the fourth question of the Query, we read this: "Do you endeavor to cultivate good will, mutual understanding, and equal opportunities for all races, creeds, and nations?" The phrase "to cultivate" is a verb metaphor, suggesting that humans are gardeners who must tend to their plots. Their crops are nothing less than good will, mutual understanding, and equal opportunity. To be a cultivator is, without doubt, to care for and tend carefully to one's plot. Gardeners use tools, but not the tools of war. They use hoes, rakes, shovels. They water, fertilize, and weed, all for the purpose of bringing their crops to life. This metaphor, as all do, implies an analogical relationship:

Gardeners		Quakers
———————	as	———————
Crops		Good Will, etc.

This metaphor and analogy of cultivation counters the final metaphor of the Query, thus staging an analogical opposition. The Query ask Quakers, finally, to examine the ways in which they live their lives and the goods they own in order "to make sure that the seeds of war are not found within them."

Just as good will, mutual understanding, and equal opportunities are plants that grow under the care of the gardener, the Query suggests that war is also a plant. Yet, it is not a foreign weed, blown in by the wind or carried in on the belly of a rabbit or on the feather of a bird. Rather, the seeds of war might come from the gardener. Thus, Quakers find themselves in a very uncomfortable position. They are asked to participate in a synecdochal relationship with the life and power that eschews war. They are asked, as part of this relationship, to tend with care to certain sorts of plants. They are reminded, however, that they themselves might carry the very thing that they are supposed to throw away: war. Thus, Quakers might follow the analogical relationship discussed previously, whereby they cultivate good will, and so on, just as gardeners would cultivate crops. However, the Quaker might also follow this relationship:

Gardener		Quaker
———————	as	———————
Bad seeds		Causes of War

The Quaker might be the gardener who tends the crops, but the Quaker, the Query suggests, might be the gardener who brings into the garden the seeds of that which will destroy all.

Such a worldview runs counter to the ways in which many people, theist or atheist, Christian or Jewish or Hindu or what-have-you, live and think. Many, for instance, glorify war. Many find the cause of war not in themselves but in others. Many despise war but see it as a necessary evil: it must be pursued so that terror, wickedness, and suffering can be stopped.

For an example of those who glorify war, one needs turn no further than the back cover of a recent translation of *The Art of War* by Sun Tzu (1971). One finds on the upper-left corner of the back cover this code: "Military History/Business." This suggests to booksellers where the book is best shelved, who the potential buyers might be. Some potential buyers are those folk interested in military history. Others are those interested in business. What is the connection between military history and business? To be sure, there are businesses that make money from war. Yet, this is not what the publisher has in mind. Rather, this publishing code implies this metaphor: business is war. Just as military historians might be interested in *The Art of War*, so too might business professionals: "War," without doubt, is the word that binds these two audiences.

Indeed, the narrative on the back cover continues this metaphor, expanding on it. Consider two sentences:

- "Sun Tzu's *The Art of War* is as timely for business people today as it was for military strategists in ancient China."
- "It is read avidly by Japanese businessmen and was touted in the movie *Wall Street* as the corporate raider's Bible."

The first sentence suggests that the theory of war is applicable to business, thus implying the metaphor, business is war, and the following analogy:

Contemporary Business
Professionals   Ancient Chinese Generals

——————————————— as ———————————————

Their Businesses   Battle

This analogy then allows a host of related metaphors to emerge. If business is war, then business CEOs become generals, vice presidents become commanders, workers become soldiers, and the competing business becomes the enemy. Unlike the Quakers, who seek to cultivate good will, equal opportunity, and mutual understanding, the company selling *The Art of War* suggests that business professionals can learn to defeat their enemies if only they take on *The Art of War*, as it is explained by Sun Tzu.

The second sentence suggests two ideas. First, *The Art of War* has a cross-cultural readership: Japanese business professionals and American business professionals. Further, if American business professionals want to compete with Japanese business professionals, they had better take heed: the Japanese see business as war and use Sun Tzu to help plan their campaigns.

Second, *The Art of War*, at least according to the Hollywood film, *Wall Street*, serves as the Bible of "corporate raiders." Those business professionals who specialize in the "takeover"—hostile or friendly—of companies are not business professionals but "raiders." They are soldiers, fighters, and warriors who use *The Art of War* to conquer others. This metaphor is used without a hint of irony, without a hint that Wall Street is fictional. We are to view *Wall Street* as a sincere depiction of the reality of business in America.

The contrast with the Quaker worldview concerning war could not be more evident, as the analogy that informs the second sentence demonstrates:

Corporate Raiders		Quakers
————————————	as	———————
The Art of War		Bible

The Quaker Queries arise from the Quaker reading of and experience with the Bible. Quakers view themselves as cultivators of a garden, guided by the Bible. Corporate takeover specialists, apparently, view themselves as "raiders," guided by *The Art of War*.

Perhaps somewhere in between the Quaker rejection of war and the corporate glorification of war rests a figure like Richard Strozzi Heckler, author of *In Search of the Warrior Spirit: Teaching Awareness Disciplines to the Green Berets* (1992). Heckler is an Aikido master and teacher, and this book chronicles his work with two Green Beret A-Teams. Aikido is a Japanese martial art that, translated, means "the way of universal harmony." The Green Beret, as is well-known, are elite special forces soldiers, part of the U.S. Army. Heckler served as part of a group hired to train Green Beret in mind/body awareness techniques. He was brought in to teach Aikido.

When Heckler agreed to participate, many people criticized his decision: Aikido, after all, "emphasizes the loving protection of life" (p. 4). Further, the Green Beret, his critics felt, "are bad people" (p. 4), "'trained killers'" (p. 3). Heckler, however, felt that he could enter into a conversation with members of the Green Beret: he could learn from them as they could learn from him. He claims that he didn't fear the soldiers, but, rather,

> those who continue to make the same terrible choices in our foreign and military policy. The men in the military after all, are the chess pieces who carry out the policy. They aren't sub-human, or even different from me. (p. 5)

Heckler's worldview is somewhere between the Quakers and the corporate world that embraces *The Art of War*. Heckler is the master of a martial art that emphasizes "loving protection." One might find this to be ironic, to be sure. After all, Aikido is a *martial* art: by definition it deals with fighting, with the martial way, the way of battle and war. Still, Heckler clearly does not embrace war. He sees Aikido as a discipline, ironic though it may be, that begets love. Moreover he criticizes those political and economic leaders who embrace war as a matter of policy: it is they whom he fears. Further still, he sees the Green Beret and other soldiers as "chess pieces."

This metaphor indicates that although the Green Beret might be warriors, they are not glorious, free-thinking, and free-acting heroes who range across the world as Heracles once did. Rather, they are pieces on a board, manipulated by wrong-headed players, players who make moves that disastrously pit soldiers against soldiers, humans against humans. Heckler does not decry war, but neither does he glamorize it, embrace it, see himself as a raider with a cause.

As has been the case throughout this book, it is important for you to find in your own lives the ways in which we figure these flashpoints, the ways in which figures permeate your lives. The following exercise will help you to explore the ways in your own life that war is figured.

❖ Exercise 6.1

1. Consider the word "war." We see it in use all the time: it fills history books, sports pages, the news. Nonetheless, most of us probably would not be able to provide quickly a concise definition. Using the *Oxford English Dictionary*, study definitions of the word "war." Are these definitions negative or positive? Then, ask yourself these two questions: Do any of these definitions involve tropes (metaphor, analogy, irony, synecdoche)? What is the worldview revealed by these definitions?

2. Find a person who has served in a war: a soldier, a nurse, a medic, or the like. Ask this person to a) tell you of his/her experiences; b) describe war in a single sentence. Reflect back on both "a" and "b." Does the person's narrative or single-sentence description involve tropes (metaphor, analogy, irony, synecdoche)? What is the worldview revealed by "a" and "b"?

3. Take a trip to your local video rental store. Ask the clerk to help you locate some "war movies." Rent one or two of these films, preferably an older war movie, like *The Sands of Iwo Jima*, and a more recent film, like *Saving Private Ryan*. Watch the films. As you watch them, ask yourself a)what tropes (metaphor, analogy, irony, synecdoche) are present?; b) what are the worldviews revealed by these tropes?

Whether you are a religious pacifist, a military historian, a business professional, a warrior, or a martial artist, you are surrounded by conflicting images of war, if not war itself. It was in a war-full world that Abraham Lincoln composed and delivered the address he presented on the occasion of his inauguration to his second term as President of the United States. This address is included in Appendix E of this book.

Abraham Lincoln's Second Inaugural Address

One of the most striking aspects of Abraham Lincoln's "Second Inaugural Address" is the synecdochal conflict at the heart of the text. One might expect that the President of the United States, who was commander-in-chief of the Union Forces, to glory in the potential victory of the Union Forces, to proclaim the absolute rightness of his army over and against the absolute wrongness of the enemy army. It is not difficult to imagine a President, inaugurated in the middle of a brutal civil war, to rally his side by proclaiming the justness of their cause and unjustness of the enemies, by making heroes of his own side, foul demons of the other.

Lincoln, however, doesn't. He opens with a story of his first inauguration, with a story about the beginning of the war. He opens not with pontification. Rather, he opens with a recounting of the synecdochal struggle at the heart of the Civil War. The Union—the "whole" in the language of tropes—was composed of at least two parts, according to Lincoln: those who sought to save it, those who sought to rend it asunder. The latter wanted to remove themselves from the part/whole relationship that marks the United States. The former wanted to maintain the whole, to keep the parts together.

Lincoln claims that as he delivered his "First Inaugural Address" "urgent agents" were "seeking to dissolve the Union." In contrast, others sought to maintain the totality of the part/whole relationship that is the United States: they were "devoted altogether to saving the Union." Both those who sought to break the whole and those who sought to save it, according to Lincoln, did so peacefully: both parts attempting to avoid war. However, war did come. One side embraced it in order to destroy the whole: "one of them would make war rather than let the nation survive." The other side "would accept war rather than let it [the whole] perish."

War is not a glorious event in Lincoln's narrative. It is, rather, a grim result, a way that a struggle over the part/whole relationship played itself out. It was not embraced, initially. The worldview of both parts of the whole preferred to act without it. However, so it seems, the strain of the synecdoche was too great for peaceful resolution. The synecdochal strain, according to Lincoln, could find resolution only through a war, unwanted but accepted and pursued.

The remainder of the "Second Inaugural Address" continues in this way. Lincoln plays the two parts against each other. Although he clearly favors one part of the whole—those who would save the Union—he doesn't speak triumphantly, doesn't demonize the Confederacy. Instead, he wonders if, indeed, the war isn't a call to humility and a chastening reminder of the mistakes that the country has made. Neither side, he tells us, can claim the favor of God. He also wonders this: Is the war the price the country must pay for slavery? This, and other elements of the speech, will become clearer as you explore them in the following exercises.

Analysis: Abraham Lincoln's Second Inaugural Address

This section provides you the opportunity to engage in your own analytic study of Lincoln's "Second Inaugural Address," included in Appendix E.

❖ *Exercise 6.2: Words and Phrases*

Consider the following five words and phrases, all drawn from the text included in Appendix E. For each, consider these questions: Is it a trope? Does it imply a trope? What kind? How does it work? Is it effective? As you answer these questions, attend to the worldviews that the words and phrases support and challenge.

1. absorbs
2. high hope
3. The Almighty
4. scourge of war
5. nation's wounds

❖ *Exercise 6.3: Sentences*

Consider these following sentences from the speech. All are drawn from the text included in Appendix E. For each sentence, mark the tropes that are present. What kind are they? How do they work? Are they effective? As you answer these questions, attend to the worldviews that the tropes support and challenge.

1. Then a statement, somewhat in detail, of a course to be pursued, seemed fitting and proper.

2. Both parties deprecated war; but one of them would *make* war rather than let the nation survive; and the other would *accept* war rather than let it perish. And the war came.

3. Both read the same Bible, and pray to the same God; and each invokes His aid against the other.

4. It may seem strange that any men should dare to ask a just God's assistance in wringing their bread from the sweat of other men's faces; but let us judge not, that we be not judged.

5. Yet, if God wills that it continue, until all the wealth piled by the bond-man's two hundred and fifty years of unrequited toil shall be sunk, and until every drop of blood drawn with the lash, shall be paid by another drawn with the sword, as was said three thousand years ago, so still it must be said "the judgments of the Lord, are true and righteous altogether."

❖ *Exercise 6.4: Topics*

Consider the following two tasks, both of which ask you to focus on Lincoln's speech included in Appendix E.

1. In a 3–4 page essay written for your class, attend to the following questions: Which trope (metaphor, analogy, synecdoche, or irony) is primary? This is to say, of all those that inform the speech, which is the most central, the one without which the speech could not survive? What is the worldview that this trope supports? What is the worldview that it challenges?

2. In a 3–4 page essay written for your class, attend to the following question: With which trope (metaphor, analogy, synecdoche, or irony) would you describe the speech? This should be your own trope, not one drawn from the text. Why this trope? What is the worldview that it supports? What is the worldview that it challenges? Does this trope indicate that you disagree with Lincoln? If so, why do you disagree? Does it indicate that you agree with Lincoln? If so, why do you agree?

❖ *Exercise 6.5: Figuring War*

The following exercise asks you to figure war. Each task requires you to take on a different guise, conduct different research. The point of each, however, is to require you to think of yourself as a member of a particular community that you want to move into a new understanding of the issue of war. Use Abraham Lincoln's "Second Inaugural Address" as a model for your speeches in the following ways:

- Use both the first-person singular, the "I," and the first-person plural, the "we," as you speak: use them to create both your own position, but also a unity with your audience.

- Make reference to key texts and events in American history, especially war and the Bible.

- Don't be afraid to make reference to the divine.

- Use very long sentences on occasion: consider the persuasive effects that long complex and compound sentences have on the audience.

- Use very formal language: no idioms, no colloquialisms, no contractions, no prepositions at the ends of phrases and sentences.

- Attend consciously to the use of tropes, especially as you revise (metaphor, analogy, irony, synecdoche).

1.   Imagine that you have been asked to speak to an audience comprising two groups that are often at odds with each other. One group is the local chapter of Peace Witness. Peace Witness is made up of area clergy (Christian and Jewish) and laity who want people in the world to "prepare for peace, not for war." The other group consists of employees of BAE Systems, a local defense contractor. This group includes company executives, engineers, and support personnel. All are happy to be with the company, for two reasons: their jobs pay well; they want to contribute to America's "defense" readiness. Two words are central to the contention between the two groups: "war" and "defense." Peace Witness claims that BAE Systems moves America further toward war. Despite claims to the contrary, BAE Systems isn't a "defense" contractor. It is a "war" contractor. After all, Peace Witness contends, why else design

highly sophisticated jet aircraft that are called "warplanes?" BAE Systems claims that it does not support war per se: it wants peace, as well. However, the company argues that America can be at peace only if potentially hostile countries see that America is ready and willing to defend itself. You have been asked to address one of the following two sets of questions: a) Is the act of preparing to defend the country implicitly an act of preparing for, indeed promoting, war? In other words, is a "defense contractor really a "war" contractor? b) Is the act of advocating for a reduction in military readiness an act of preparing for, indeed promoting, war? In other words, is the "peace movement" really a "war movement?" Compose a five-minute written speech that answers one of these questions. Use no visual aids.

2. Imagine that you have been asked to speak to a group of Boy Scout leaders at a spring retreat. They have asked you to address a controversial marker at their summer camp. On a bluff high above the central meeting area is a large cross. It was placed there in 1973 by a Scout leader in order to commemorate a friend and fellow Scout leader who had served as a soldier, and had been killed in the Vietnam War. One group of Scout leaders wants the cross removed. They argue that it promotes militarism in the Scouting movement, that it glorifies war. Another group wants to keep the cross. They argue that the Scout leader who died was a hero and should be remembered as such. They also argue that Scouting, in part, is about God and Country, as one of highest badges is called. The cross reminds Scouts at the summer camp what is at the heart of the Scouting experience. Compose a five-minute written speech that addresses this question: Should the cross be removed, or not? Use no visual aids.

Appendix A

W.E.B. Du Bois
Editorials on Education

W.E.B. Du Bois was one of America's pre-eminent intellectuals and activists. A prolific writer and speaker, he was also the founding editor of The Crisis, *the journal of the National Association for the Advancement of Colored People (NAACP). He edited* The Crisis *for over 20 years, shaping it into the country's foremost periodical on issues of race. The three editorials included here were written by Du Bois and published in the pages of* The Crisis. *They are also reprinted in* The Complete Published Works of W.E.B. Du Bois: Writings in Periodicals Edited by W.E.B. Du Bois: Selections from The Crisis *(vol. 1, ed. and comp. Herbert Aptheker, Millwood, New York: Kraus-Thomson, Ltd., 1983, pp. 36–37, 103–105, and 342, respectively).*

"Education" *The Crisis*

Consider this argument: Education is the training of men for life. The best training is experience, but if we depended entirely upon this each generation would begin where the last began and civilization could not advance.

We must then depend largely on oral and written tradition and on such bits of typical experience as we can arrange for the child's guidance to life.

More than that, children must be trained in the technique of earning a living and doing their part of the world's work.

But no training in technique must forget that the object of education is the child and not the thing he makes.

Moreover, a training simply in technique will not do because general intelligence is needed for any trade, and the technique of trades changes.

Indeed, by the careful training of intelligence and ability, civilization is continually getting rid of the hardest and most exhaustive toil, and giving it over to machines, leaving human beings freer for higher pursuits and self-development.

Hence, colored people in educating their children should be careful:

First: To conserve and select ability, giving to their best minds higher college training.

Second: They should endeavor to give all their children the largest possible amount of general training and intelligence before teaching them the technique of a particular trade, remembering that the object of all true education is not to make men carpenters, but to make carpenters men.

Is not this reasoning sound? Could you imagine an educator of any experience who would take material exception to it? Would you call it revolutionary or in the nature of a "personal" attack?

Certainly not.

Yet this very argument, with illustrations and emphasis delivered to some seven hundred apparently well-pleased folk in Indianapolis, has had the most astounding results. The Indianapolis *Star* in a leading editorial denounced it as "dangerous!"

A leading white philanthropist of abolition forbears considered it not only "misleading" and "mischievous" but a covert and damaging personal attack!

The supervisor of the colored schools of Indianapolis wrote to express regret that the lecture had seemed to attack his school curriculum and ideals, and the assistant superintendent of schools in the District of Columbia hastens to give advice!

Yet where is the flaw in the argument?

There is no flaw, but there are serious flaws in the thinking of some of these critics.

The first flaw is the naïve assumption that the paraphernalia of a school shows the education it is imparting. If some people see a Greek book and a cap and gown, they conclude that the boy between them is receiving a higher education. But is he? That depends. If other people see a hammer, a saw and a cook book, they conclude that the boy who uses them is being trained in intelligence, ability and the earning of a living. But is he? That depends.

When the proud principal of a school shows workshop and kitchen, table and pie, one may be interested, but one is no more convinced than when another shows an array of Greek roots and rounded phrases. One must merely remark: The end of education is neither the table nor the phrase—it is the boy; what kind of boys are you training here? Are they boys quickened in intelligence, with some knowledge of the world they live in? Are they trained in such ways as to discover their true bent and ability, and to be intelligently guided to the choice of a life work? Then your system is right. Otherwise it is wrong, and not all the gingham dresses in Indiana will justify it.

The second flaw is the more or less conscious determination of certain folk to use the American public-school system for the production of laborers who will do the work they want done. To them Indianapolis exists for the sake of its factories and not the factories for the sake of Indianapolis. They want dinners, chairs and motor cars, and they want them cheap; therefore use the public schools to train servants, carpenters and mechanics. It does not occur to them to think of workingmen as existing for their own sakes. What with impudent maids, and half-trained workingmen, they are tired of democracy; they want caste; a place for everybody and everybody in his father's place with themselves on top, and "Niggers" at the bottom where they belong. To such folk the problem of education is strikingly simple. To teach the masses to work; show them how to do things; increase their output; give them intelligence, of course; but this as a means, not as an end, and be careful of too much of it. Of course, if a meteoric genius bursts his birth's invidious bar, let him escape, but keep up the bars, and as most men are fools, treat them and train them as such.

It was such darkened counsels as these that brought the French Revolution. It is such mad logic as this that is at the bottom of the social unrest to-day.

The lecturer came to Indianapolis not to criticise, but to warn—not to attack, but to make straight the way of the Lord. He is no despiser of common humble toil; God forbid! He and his fathers before him have worked with their hands at the lowliest occupations and he honors any honest toilers at any task; but he makes no mistake here. It is the toilers that he honors, not the task—the man and not the Thing. The Thing may or may not be honorable—the man always is.

Yet the despising of men is growing and the caste spirit is rampant in the land; it is laying hold of the public schools and it has the colored public schools by the throat, North, East, South, and West. Beware of it, my brothers and dark sisters; educate your children. Give them the broadest and highest education possible; train them to the limit of their ability, if you work your hands to the bone in doing it. See that your child gets, not the highest task, but the task best fitted to his ability, whether it be digging dirt or painting landscapes; remembering that our recognition as common folk by the world depends on the number of men of ability we produce—not great geniuses, but efficient thinkers and doers in all lines. Never forget that if we ever compel the world's respect, it will be by virtue of our heads and not our heels.

—"Education" *The Crisis* 4 (June 1912): 74–76.

The Persistent Onslaught

The quiet insidious attempt to keep the mass of Negroes in America in just sufficient ignorance to render them incapable of realizing their power or resisting the position of inferiority into which the bulk of the nation is determined to thrust them was never stronger than to-day. Let us not be deceived. It is true that our illiteracy has decreased enormously and is decreasing and that the number of our children reported to be in school is larger than ever before. At the same time our illiteracy has not decreased as quickly as it might have and it is doubtful if the proportion of our population in school is as large to-day as it was ten or twenty years ago. As a race we are still kept in ignorance far below the average standard of this nation and of the present age, and the ideals set before our children in most cases are far below their possibilities and reasonable promise.

This is true not by accident but by design, and by the design not so much of the laboring white masses of the nation but rather by the design of rich and intelligent people, and particularly by those who masquerade as the Negroes' "friends." Their attack on real education for Negroes is in reality one with their attack on education for working men in general and this is part of the great modern attack upon democracy.

Of course, the movement masquerades as industrial and vocational training in an age which is preeminently industrial and busy. It is thus difficult for the average colored man to descry its persistent and tremendous dangers to our ultimate survival as a race and as American citizens.

The Basic Injustice
No one denies that beneath the basic demand for industrial and vocational training lies truth and fundamental truth, but that on this truth is being built to-day a superstructure of falsehood and injustice also too clear to the thinker. It is the duty of all men to work and this work usually renders a service to the community for which the community is willing to pay with services and materials in return. Sometimes, to be sure, the community does not recognize the value of work; sometimes it pays ridiculous pittances for work of the very highest value and [. . .][†] on the other hand it again and again pays extortionate returns for services that are negligible or even absolute disservice. Nevertheless the average man must be trained for work which the average community will reward with a living wage. In these days of intricate technique such training cannot be acquired by chance or as a side issue or as an after thought. It must form an integral part of every person's education. "Therefore," says the principal of the school with the largest Negro attendance in Harlem, "I am going to train these Negroes as cooks and gardeners."

The Basic Fallacy
But wait; is work the object of life or is life the object of work? Are men to earn a living or simply to live for the sake of working? Is there any justice in making a particular body of men the drudges of society, destined for the worst work under the worst conditions and at the lowest pay, simply because a majority of their fellow men for more or less indefinite and superficial reasons do not like them? Manifestly life, and abundant life, is the object of industry and we teach men to earn a living in order that their industry may administer to their own lives and the lives of their fellows. If, therefore, any human being has large ability it is not only for his advantage but for the advantage of all society that he be put to the work that he can do best. To assume that ability is to be measured by so-called racial characteristics—by color, by hair, or by stature is not only ridiculous but dangerous. To-day we can afford to look carefully day are for men and men for machines,^{††} while on the other hand

---

[†] A phrase of approximately ten words has been removed. It appears to have been reprinted from a later edition.

^{††} This misphrasing is the original.

because of the mechanical and industrial age through which we have passed there is a grave lack of deep intelligence and character. While then we teach men to earn a living, that teaching is incidental and subordinate to the larger training of intelligence in human beings and to the largest development of self-realization in men. Those who would deny this to the Negro race are enemies of mankind.

The Result

The result of limiting the education of Negroes under the mask of fitting them for work is the slow strangulation of the Negro college. Howard today is dependent upon the precarious support of the majority in Congress; Fisk has an endowment which looks ridiculous beside that of Hampton and Tuskegee. Atlanta has almost no endowment. None of the five major Negro colleges have today any solid financial prospect for growth and development. Not only that but they are regularly sneered at by men who dared not raise their arguments above a sneer. We hear again and again repeated the usual lie that these colleges are persisting in the curriculum of fifty years ago. As a matter of fact practically all of these colleges are conforming to the standard of education as laid down by the highest authorities in this country. What they are really asked to do is to adopt a course of study which does not conform to modern standards, which no modern system of education will recognize and which condemns the student who takes it to end his education in a blind alley. It is the unforgivable sin of some of the greatest so-called industrial schools that the boy who is induced to take their course is absolutely unfitted thereby from continuing his education at a recognized modern institution. This is a crime against childhood for which any nation ought to be ashamed.

Who are the men who are planning the new Negro curriculum? Are they educational experts learned in the theory and practise of training youth? No, most of them never taught a child or held any responsible place in a school system or gave the subject any serious study. Are they friends of the Negro desiring his best interests and development? No, they are friends of the white South and stand openly committed to any demand of the white South.

The latest attack on Negro education comes from Philadelphia. Very adroitly and cunningly the Negroes have been massed in segregated schools. Now "industrial training" is to be introduced *in the Negro schools* and a representative of a leading southern industrial school is on hand to advise!

Do Negroes oppose this because they are ashamed of having their children trained to work? Certainly not. But they know that if their children are compelled to cook and sew when they ought to be learning to read, write and cipher, they will not be able to enter the high school or go to college as the white children are doing. It is a deliberate despicable attempt to throttle the Negro child before he knows enough to protest.

The Excuse
Even in industrial training the white authorities are persistently dishonest. They will not train our children in good paying trades and respectable vocations. They want them to be servants and menials. The excuse which is continually brought forward, particularly in the North, is that there is "no opening" for them in the higher ranges of the industrial world! For this reason opportunities even for the best industrial training are persistently denied colored students. Trade schools in many of the large cities have the habit of forcing colored students who apply into the courses for domestic service or sewing on the plea that millinery, carpentry and various lines of mechanical work offer no opportunity for colored folk. Surely this reduces the argument for industrial training to rank absurdity and the cause of real, honest industrial training deserves more sensible treatment than this.

Our Attitude
In all these arguments and actions there blazes one great and shining light: the persistent army of Negro boys and girls pushing through high school and college continues to increase. Negro mothers and fathers are not being entirely deceived. They know that intelligence and self-development are the only means by which the Negro is to win his way in the modern world. They persist in pushing their children on through the highest courses. May they always continue to do so; and may the bright, fine faces on these pages be inspiration to thousands of other boys and girls in the coming years to resist the contemptible temptation so persistently laid before this race to train its children simply as menials and scavengers.

—"Education" *The Crisis* 10 (July 1915): 132–33, 136.

There is a widespread feeling that a school is a machine. You insert a child at 9 a.m. and extract it at 4 p.m., improved and standardized with parts of Grade IV, first term. In truth, school is a desperate duel between new souls and old to pass on facts and methods and dreams from a dying world to a world in birth pains without letting either teacher or taught lose for a moment faith and interest. It is hard work. Often, most often, it is a futile failure. It is never wholly a success without the painstaking help of the parent.

Yet I know Negroes, thousands of them, who never visit the schools where their children go; who do not know the teachers or what they teach or what they are supposed to teach; who do not consult the authorities on matters of discipline—do not know who or what is in control of the schools or how much money is needed or received.

Oh, we have our excuses! The teachers do not want us around. They do not welcome co-operation. Colored patrons especially may invite insult or laughter. All true in some cases. Yet the best schools and the best teachers pray for and welcome the continuous and intelligent co-operation of parents. And the worst schools need it and must be made to realize their need.

There has been much recent discussion among Negroes as to the merits of mixed and segregated schools. It is said that our children are neglected in mixed schools. "Let us have our own schools. How else can we explain the host of colored High School graduates in Washington, and the few in Philadelphia?" Easily. In Washington, colored parents are intensely interested in their schools and have for years followed and watched and criticized them. In Philadelphia, the colored people have evinced no active interest save in *colored* schools and there is no colored High School.

Save the great principle of democracy and equal opportunity and fight segregation by wealth, class or race or color, not by yielding to it but by watching, visiting and voting in all school matters, organizing parents and children and bringing every outside aid and influence to co-operate with teachers and authorities.

In the North with mixed schools unless colored patrons take intelligent, continuous and organized interest in the schools which their children attend, the children will be neglected, treated unjustly, discouraged and balked of their natural self-expression and ambition. Do not allow this. Supervise your children's schools.

In the South unless the patrons know and visit the schools and keep up continuous, intelligent agitation, the teachers will be sycophants, the studies designed to make servant girls, and the funds stolen by the white trustees.

—"Education" *The Crisis* 24 (October 1922): 252.

Appendix B

National Conference of Catholic Bishops

Preface to *Economic Justice for All: Pastoral Letter on Catholic Social Teaching and the U.S. Economy*

Published in 1986, Economic Justice For All represents a long-standing tradition in the Christian Church: the pastoral letter. Primarily written for members of the Catholic Church, Economic Justice For All intends to lead church members to a new understanding of the economy in light of the teachings of the Roman Catholic Church. Excerpted here are Sections 1–22 from the Preface of the letter.

Brothers and Sisters in Christ:

1. We are believers called to follow Our Lord Jesus Christ and proclaim his Gospel in the midst of a complex and powerful economy. This reality poses both opportunities and responsibilities for Catholics in the United States. Our faith calls us to measure this economy, not by what it produces, but also by how it touches human life and whether it protects or undermines the dignity of the human person. Economic decisions have human consequences and moral content; they help or hurt people,

strengthen or weaken family life, advance or diminish the quality of justice in our land.

2. This is why we have written *Economic Justice for All: A Pastoral Letter on Catholic Social Teaching and the U.S. Economy*. This letter is a personal invitation to Catholics to use the resources of our faith, the strength of our economy, and the opportunities of our democracy to shape a society that better protects the dignity and basic rights of our sisters and brothers, both in this land and around the world.

3. This pastoral letter has been a work of careful inquiry, wide consultation, and prayerful discernment. The letter has been greatly enriched by this process of listening and refinement. We offer this introductory pastoral message to Catholics in the United States seeking to live their faith in the marketplace—in homes, offices, factories, and schools; on farms and ranches; in boardrooms and union halls; in service agencies and legislative chambers. We seek to explain why we wrote the pastoral letter, to introduce its major themes, and to share our hopes for the dialogue and action it might generate.

Why We Write

4. We write to share our teaching, to raise questions, to challenge one another to live our faith in the world. We write as heirs of the biblical prophets who summon us "to do right, and to love goodness, and to walk humbly with your God" (Mi 6:8). We write as followers of Jesus who told us in the Sermon on the Mount: "Blessed are the poor in spirit. . . . Blessed are the meek. . . . Blessed are they who hunger and thirst for righteousness. . . . You are the salt of the earth. . . . You are the light of the world" (Mt 5:1–6, 13–14). These words challenge us not only as believers but also as consumers, citizens, workers, and owners. In the parable of the Last Judgment, Jesus said, "For I was hungry and you gave me food, I was thirsty and you gave me drink. . . . As often as you did it for one of my least brothers, you did it for me" (Mt 25:35–40). The challenge for us is to discover in our own place and time what it means to be "poor in spirit" and "the salt of the earth" and what it means to serve "the least among us" and to "hunger and thirst for righteousness."

5. Followers of Christ must avoid a tragic separation between faith and everyday life. They can neither shirk their earthly duties nor, as the

Second Vatican Council declared, "immerse [them]selves in earthly activities as if these latter were utterly foreign to religion, and religion were nothing more than the fulfillment of acts of worship and the observance of a few moral obligations" (*Pastoral Constitution on the Church in the Modern World*, no. 43).

6. Economic life raises important social and moral questions for each of us and for the society as a whole. Like family life, economic life is one of the chief areas where we live out our faith, love our neighbor, confront temptation, fulfill God's creative design, and achieve holiness. Our economic activity in factory, field, office, or shop feeds our families—or feeds our anxieties. It exercises our talents—or wastes them. It raises our hopes—or crushes them. It brings us into cooperation with others—or sets us at odds. The Second Vatican Council instructs us "to preach the message of Christ in such a way that the light of the Gospel will shine on all activities of the faithful" (*Pastoral Constitution*, no. 43). In this case, we are trying to look at economic life through the eyes of faith, applying traditional church teaching to the U.S. economy.

7. In our letter, we write as pastors, not public officials. We speak as moral teachers, not economic technicians. We seek not to make some political or ideological point but to lift up the human and ethical dimensions of economic life, aspects too often neglected in public discussion. We bring to this task a dual heritage of Catholic social teaching and traditional American values.

8. As *Catholics*, we are heirs of a long tradition of thought and action on the moral dimensions of economic activity. The life and words of Jesus and the teaching of his Church call us to serve those in need and to work actively for social and economic justice. As a community of believers, we know that our faith is tested by the quality of justice among us, that we can best measure our life together by how the poor and the vulnerable are treated. This is not a new concern for us. It is as old as the Hebrew prophets, as compelling as the Sermon on the Mount, and as current as the powerful voice of Pope John Paul II defending the dignity of the human person.

9. As *Americans*, we are grateful for the gift of freedom and committed to the dream of "liberty and justice for all." This nation, blessed with extraordinary resources, has provided an unprecedented standard of living for millions of people. We are proud of the strength, productivity, and creativity of our economy, but we also remember those who

have been left behind in our progress. We believe that we honor our history best by working for the day when all our sisters and brothers share adequately in the American dream.

10. As bishops, in proclaiming the Gospel for these times we also manage institutions, balance budgets, meet payrolls. In this we see the human face of our economy. We feel the hurts and hopes of our people. We feel the pain of our sisters and brothers who are poor, unemployed, homeless, living on the edge. The poor and vulnerable are on our doorsteps, in our parishes, in our service agencies, and in our shelters. We see too much hunger and injustice, too much suffering and despair, both in our country and around the world.

11. As pastors, we also see the decency, generosity, and vulnerability of our people. We see the struggles of ordinary families to make ends meet and to provide a better future for their children. We know the desire of managers, professionals, and business people to shape what they do by what they believe. It is the faith, good will, and generosity of our people that gives us hope as we write this letter.

Principal Themes of the Pastoral Letter

12. The pastoral letter is not a blueprint for the American economy. It does not embrace any particular theory of how the economy works, nor does it attempt to resolve disputes between different schools of economic thought. Instead, our letter turns to Scripture and to the social teaching of the Church. There, we discover what our economic life must serve, what standards it must meet. Let us examine some of these basic moral principles.

13. *Every economic decision and institution must be judged in light of whether it protects or undermines the dignity of the human person.* The pastoral letter begins with the human person. We believe the person is sacred—the clearest reflection of God among us. Human dignity comes from God, not from nationality, race, sex, economic status, or any human accomplishment. We judge any economic system by what it does *for* and *to* people and by how it permits all to *participate* in it. The economy should serve people, not the other way around.

14. *Human dignity can be realized and protected only in community.* In our teaching, the human person is not only sacred but social. How we

organize our society—in economics and politics, in law and policy—directly affects human dignity and the capacity of individuals to grow in community. The obligation to "love our neighbor" has an individual dimension, but it also requires a broader social commitment to the common good. We have many partial ways to measure and debate the health of our economy: Gross National Product, per capita income, stock market prices, and so forth. The Christian vision of economic life looks beyond them all and asks, Does economic life enhance or threaten our life together as a community?

15. *All people have a right to participate in the economic life of society.* Basic justice demands that people be assured a minimum level of participation in the economy. It is wrong for a person or a group to be excluded unfairly or to be unable to participate or contribute to the economy. For example, people who are both able and willing, but cannot get a job are deprived of the participation that is so vital to human development. For, it is through employment that most individuals and families meet their material needs, exercise their talents, and have an opportunity to contribute to the larger community. Such participation has a special significance in our tradition because we believe that it is a means by which we join in carrying forward God's creative activity.

16. *All members of society have a special obligation to the poor and vulnerable.* From the Scriptures and church teaching, we learn that the justice of a society is tested by the treatment of the poor. The justice that was the sign of God's covenant with Israel was measured by how the poor and unprotected—the widow, the orphan, and the stranger—were treated. The kingdom that Jesus proclaimed in his word and ministry excludes no one. Throughout Israel's history and in early Christianity, the poor are agents of God's transforming power. "The Spirit of the Lord is upon me, therefore he has anointed me. He has sent me to bring glad tidings to the poor" (Lk 4:18). This was Jesus' first public utterance. Jesus takes the side of those most in need. In the Last Judgment, so dramatically described in St. Matthew's Gospel, we are told that we will be judged according to how we respond to the hungry, the thirsty, the naked, the stranger. As followers of Christ, we are challenged to make a fundamental "option for the poor"—to speak for the voiceless, to defend the defenseless, to assess life styles, policies, and social institutions in terms of their impact on the poor. This "option for the poor" does not mean pitting one group against another, but rather, strengthening the

whole community by assisting those who are the most vulnerable. As Christians, we are called to respond to the needs of *all* our brothers and sisters, but those with the greatest needs require the greatest response.

17. *Human rights are the minimum conditions for life in community.* In Catholic teaching, human rights include not only civil and political rights but also economic rights. As Pope John XXIII declared, "all people have a right to life, food, clothing, shelter, rest, medical care, education, and employment." This means that when people are without a chance to earn a living, and must go hungry and homeless, they are being denied basic rights. Society must ensure that these rights are protected. In this way, we will ensure that the minimum conditions of economic justice are met for all our sisters and brothers.

18. *Society as a whole, acting through public and private institutions, has the moral responsibility to enhance human dignity and protect human rights.* In addition to the clear responsibility of private institutions, government has an essential responsibility in this area. This does not mean that government has the primary or exclusive role, but it does have a positive moral responsibility in safeguarding human rights and ensuring that the minimum conditions of human dignity are met for all. In a democracy, government is a means by which we can act together to protect what is important to us and to promote our common values.

19. These six moral principles are not the only ones presented in the pastoral letter, but they give an overview of the moral vision that we are trying to share. This vision of economic life cannot exist in a vacuum; it must be translated into concrete measures. Our pastoral letter spells out some specific applications of Catholic moral principles. We call for a new national commitment to full employment. We say it is a social and moral scandal that one of every seven Americans is poor, and we call for concerted efforts to eradicate poverty. The fulfillment of the basic needs of the poor is of the highest priority. We urge that all economic policies be evaluated in light of their impact on the life and stability of the family. We support measures to halt the loss of family farms and to resist the growing concentration in the ownership of agricultural resources. We specify ways in which the United States can do far more to relieve the plight of poor nations and assist in their development. We also reaffirm church teaching on the rights of workers, collective bargaining, private property, subsidiarity, and equal opportunity.

20. We believe that the recommendations in our letter are reasonable and balanced. In analyzing the economy, we reject ideological extremes and start from the fact that ours is a "mixed" economy, the product of a long history of reform and adjustment. We know that some of our specific recommendations are controversial. As bishops, we do not claim to make these prudential judgments with the same kind of authority that marks our declarations of principle. But, we feel obliged to teach by example how Christians can undertake concrete analysis and make specific judgments on economic issues. The Church's teachings cannot be left at the level of appealing generalities.

21. In the pastoral letter, we suggest that the time has come for a "New American Experiment"—to implement economic rights, to broaden the sharing of economic power, and to make economic decisions more accountable to the common good. This experiment can create new structures of economic partnership and participation within firms at the regional level, for the whole nation, and across borders.

22. Of course, there are many aspects of the economy the letter does not touch, and there are basic questions it leaves to further exploration. There are also many specific points on which men and women of good will may disagree. We look for a fruitful exchange among differing viewpoints. We pray only that all will take to heart the urgency of our concerns; that together we will test our views by the Gospel and the Church's teaching; and that we will listen to other voices in a spirit of mutual respect and open dialogue.

—National Conference of Catholic Bishops. Washington, D.C.: United States Catholic Conference, 1986, pp. v–xvi.

Appendix C

Sojourner Truth
"A'n't I a Woman"

Delivered as an oral performance, there is no extant written version of "A'n't I A Woman?" As a result, many versions have appeared since Truth delivered her speech at a women's rights convention in Akron, Ohio, in 1851. One of the most prominent is a version that appeared in the Anti-Slavery Bugle *on June 21, 1851. This version now appears in various published sources, including Jeffrey C. Stewart's "Introduction" to* Narrative of Sojourner Truth; A Bondswoman of Olden Time, With a History of Her Labors and Correspondence Drawn from Her "Book of Life" *(Oxford University Press, 1991, p. xxxiii) and Sojourner Truth's* Narrative of Sojourner Truth *(ed. Margaret Washington, New York: Vintage, 1993, pp. 117–118). Truth's speech was rendered by the* Anti-Slavery Bugle *into near-standard edited American English, whether or not she actually spoke this type of English. Perhaps the most prominent version of Truth's speech is the one recorded in 1863 by Frances Dana Gage, who helped organize the Akron convention at which the speech was first delivered. Gage's version turns Truth into a woman who speaks a Southern Black English dialect, even though Truth was a slave in New York State. Gage's version is printed here, despite the racist undercurrent: she makes Truth into a "black" speaker. This fact alone makes it interesting: readers might want to query the ways in which Gage's version might or might not be implicated in racism. Gage's version*

now appears in a number of places, among them such World Wide Web sites as www.courses.washington.edu/spcmu/speeches/ sojournertruth.htm (accessed 3/26/01) and www.sojourn- ertruth.org/Library/Speeches/A'n'tIAWoman.html (accessed 3/26/01). It also appears in Narrative of Sojourner Truth; A Bondswoman of Olden Time, With a History of Her Labors and Correspondence Drawn from Her "Book of Life" *(Oxford University Press, 1991, pp. 131–135), and* Voices of Multicultural America: Notable Speeches Delivered by African, Asian, Hispanic and Native Americans, *1790–1995 (ed. Deborah Gillan Straub, New York: Gale Research, 1996, pp. 1189–1191). Gage's version has also been rendered with the "dialect markers." For this version see* Man Cannot Speak for Her *(v. 2, comp. Karlyn Kohrs Campbell, New York: Greenwood Press, 1989, pp. 99–102). The version printed here is from* History of Woman Suffrage *(ed. Elizabeth Cody Stanton, Susan B. Anthony, and Matilda Joslyn Gage, vol. 1, New York: Fowler and Wells, 1881, pp. 115–117; reprint, New York: Arno Press, 1969).*

The leaders of the movement trembled on seeing a tall, gaunt black woman in a gray dress and white turban, surmounted with an uncouth sun-bonnet, march deliberately into the church, walk with the air of a queen up the aisle, and take her seat upon the pulpit steps. A buzz of dis- approbation was heard all over the house, and there fell on the listening ear, "An abolition affair!" "Woman's rights and niggers!" "I told you so!" "Go it, darkey!"

I chanced on that occasion to wear my first laurels in public life as president of the meeting. At my request order was restored and the business of the Convention went on. Morning, afternoon, and evening exercises came and went. Through all these sessions old Sojourner, quiet and reticent as the "Lybian Statue," sat crouched against the wall on the corner of the pulpit stairs, her sun-bonnet shading her eyes, her elbows on her knees, her chin resting upon her broad, hard palms. At intermission she was busy selling "The Life of Sojourner Truth," a nar- rative of her own strange and adventurous life. Again and again, tim- orous and trembling ones came to me and said, with earnestness, "Don't let her speak, Mrs. Gage, it will ruin us. Every newspaper in the land will have our cause mixed up with abolition and niggers and we shall be utterly denounced." My only answer was, "We shall see when the time comes."

The second day the work waxed warm. Methodist, Baptist, Episcopal, Presbyterian, and Universalist ministers came in to hear and discuss the resolutions presented. One claimed superior rights and privileges for man, on the ground of "superior intellect"; another, because of the "manhood of Christ; if God had desired the equality of woman, He would have given some token of His will through the birth, life and death of the Saviour." Another gave us a theological view of the "sin of the first mother."

There were very few women in those days who dared to "speak in meeting"; and the august teachers of the people were seemingly getting the best of us, while the boys in the galleries, and the sneerers among the pews, were hugely enjoying the discomfiture, as they supposed, of the "strong-minded." Some of the tender-skinned friends were on the point of losing dignity, and the atmosphere betokened a storm. When, slowly from her seat in the corner rose Sojourner Truth, who, till now, had scarcely lifted her head. "Don't let her speak!" gasped half a dozen in my ear. She moved slowly and solemnly to the front, laid her old bonnet at her feet, and turned her great speaking eyes to me. There was a hissing sound of disapprobation above and below. I rose and announced "Sojourner Truth," and begged the audience to keep silence for a few moments.

The tumult subsided at once, and every eye was fixed on this almost Amazon form, which stood nearly six feet high, head erect, and eyes piercing the upper air like one in a dream. At her first word there was a profound hush. She spoke in deep tones, which, though not loud, reached every ear in the house, and away through the throng at the doors and windows.

"Wall, chilern, whar dar is so much racket dar must be somethin' out o' kilter. I tink dat 'twixt de niggers of de Souf and de womin at de Norf, all talkin' 'bout rights, de white men will be in a fix pretty soon. But what's all dis here talkin' 'bout?

"Dat man ober dar say dat womin needs to be helped into carriages, and lifted ober ditches, and to hab de best place everywhar. Nobody eber helps me into carriages, or ober mudpuddles, or gibs me any best place!" And raising herself to her full height, and her voice to a pitch like rolling thunder, she asked, "And a'n't I a woman? Look at me! Look at my arm! [and she bared her right arm to the shoulder, showing her tremendous muscular power]. "I have ploughed, and planted, and gathered into barns, and no man could head me! And a'n't I a woman? I could work as much and eat as much as a man—when I could get it—and bear de lash as well! And a'n't' I a woman? I have borne thirteen chilern, and seen 'em mos' all sold off to slavery, and when I cried out with my mother's grief, none but Jesus heard me! And a'n't I a woman?

"Den dey talks 'bout dis ting in de head; what dis dey call it?" ("Intellect," whispered some one near). "Dat's it, honey. What's dat got to do wid womin's rights or nigger's rights? If my cup won't hold but a pint, and yourn holds a quart, wouldn't ye be mean not to let me have my little half-measure full?" And she pointed her significant finger, and sent a keen glance at the minister who had made the argument. The cheering was long and loud.

"Den dat little man in black dar, he say women can't have as much rights as men, 'cause Christ wan't a woman! Whar did your Christ come from?" Rolling thunder couldn't have stilled that crowd, as did those deep, wonderful tones, as she stood there with outstretched arms and eyes of fire. Raising her voice still louder, she repeated, "Whar did your Christ come from? From God and a woman! Man had nothin' to do wid Him." Oh, what a rebuke that was to that little man.

Turning again to another objector, she took up the defense of Mother Eve. I cannot follow her through it all. It was pointed, and witty, and solemn; eliciting at almost every sentence deafening applause; and she ended by asserting, "If de fust woman God ever made was strong enough to turn de world upside down all alone, dese women togedder [and she glanced her eye over the platform] ought to be able to turn it back, and get it right side up again! And now dey is asking to do it, de men better let 'em." Long-continued cheering greeted this. "'Bleeged to ye for hearin' on me, and now ole Sojourner han't got nothin' more to say."

Amid roars of applause, she returned to her corner, leaving more than one of us with streaming eyes, and hearts beating with gratitude. She had taken us up in her strong arms and carried us safely over the slough of difficulty turning the whole tide in our favor. I have never in my life seen anything like the magical influence that subdued the mob-bish spirit of the day, and turned the sneers and jeers of an excited crowd into notes of respect and admiration. Hundreds rushed up to shake hands with her, and congratulate the glorious old mother, and bid her Godspeed on her mission of "testifyin' agin concerning the wickedness of this 'ere people."

—Sojourner Truth, as recorded by Francis Gage

Appendix D

Gary Snyder
"Breasts" and "For All"

Gary Snyder is a West Coast poet, well-known for his involvement in two major literary movements. The first was the San Francisco Renaissance, the second the Beat. Snyder has published numerous books, among them the Pulitzer Prize–winning volume of poetry, Turtle Island *(New Directions, 1975).*

"Breasts"

That which makes milk can't
          help but concentrate
Out of the food of the world,
Right up to the point
          where we suck it,
Poison, too

But the breast is a filter—
The poison stays there, in the flesh.
Heavy metals in traces
          deadly molecules hooked up in strings
          that men dreamed of;
Never found in the world til today.
          (in your bosom
          petrochemical complex
          astray)

So we celebrate breasts
We all love to kiss them
   —they're like philosophers!
Who hold back the bitter in mind
To let the more tasty
Wisdom slip through
   for the little ones.
   who can't take the poison so young.

The work that comes later
After child-raising
For the real self to be,
Is to then burn the poison away.
Flat breasts, tired bodies,
That will snap like old leather,
   tough enough
   for a few more good days,

And the glittering eyes,
Old mother,
Old father,
   are gay.

"For All"

Ah to be alive
   on a mid-September morn
   fording a stream
   barefoot, pants rolled up,
   holding boots, pack on,
   sunshine, ice in the shallows,
   northern rockies.

Rustle and shimmer of icy creek waters
stones turned underfoot, small and hard as toes
   cold nose dripping
   singing inside
   creek music, heart music,
   smell of sun on gravel.

   I pledge allegiance

I pledge allegiance to the soil
   of Turtle Island,

and to the beings who thereon dwell
    one ecosystem
    in diversity
    under the sun
With joyful interpenetration for all.

—from *Axe Handles* by Gary Snyder (North Point Press, 1983).

Appendix E

Abraham Lincoln
Second Inaugural Address
Saturday, March 4, 1865

Abraham Lincoln delivered his second Inaugural Address as the Civil War was still hot but moving toward its end. This address shows Lincoln to be man at once political and religious, willing to weave theology and political commentary together. The speech is available through any number sources, print and electronic. One such print version is Abraham Lincoln: Selected Speeches, Messages, and Letters *(ed. T. Harry Williams New York: Rinehart and Company, 1957). Others are* A Treasury of the World's Great Speeches *(comp. and ed. Houston Peterson, New York: Simon and Schuster, 1954, pp. 523–525) and* Presidential Documents: The Speeches, Proclamations, and Policies that Have Shaped the Nation from Washington to Clinton *(ed. J.F. Watts and Fred L. Israel, New York: Routledge, 2000, pp. 138–140). Among the many World Wide Web sites that publish the speech are these at colleges and universities: The Avalon Project at Yale Law School (accessed 3/26/01): www.yale.edu/lawweb/avalon/presiden/inaug/lincoln2.htm; The Program in Presidential Rhetoric sponsored by the Center for Presidential Studies and the Department of Speech Communication at Texas A&M (accessed 3/26/01): www.tamu.edu/scom/pres/pres.html; The University of Oklahoma Law*

Center (accessed 3/26/01): www.law.ou.edu/hist/lincoln2.html. The version printed here is from The Atlantic *online: www.theatlantic. com/issues/99sep/9909lineaddress.htm (accessed 6/11/01).*

Fellow-Countrymen:

At this second appearing to take the oath of the presidential office, there is less occasion for an extended address than there was at the first. Then a statement, somewhat in detail, of a course to be pursued, seemed fitting and proper. Now, at the expiration of four years, during which public declarations have been constantly called forth on every point and phase of the great contest which still absorbs the attention, and engrosses the energies of the nation, little that is new could be presented. The progress of our arms, upon which all else chiefly depends, is as well known to the public as to myself; and it is, I trust, reasonably satisfactory and encouraging to all. With high hope for the future, no prediction in regard to it is ventured.

On the occasion corresponding to this four years ago, all thoughts were anxiously directed to an impending civil-war. All dreaded it—all sought to avert it. While the inaugural address was being delivered from this place, devoted altogether to *saving* the Union without war, insurgent agents were in the city seeking to *destroy* it without war—seeking to dissolve the Union, and divide effects, by negotiation. Both parties deprecated war; but one of them would *make* war rather than let the nation survive; and the other would *accept* war rather than let it perish. And the war came.

One-eighth of the whole population were colored slaves, not distributed generally over the Union, but localized in the Southern part of it. These slaves constituted a peculiar and powerful interest. All knew that this interest was, somehow, the cause of the war. To strengthen, perpetuate, and extend this interest was the object for which the insurgents would rend the Union, even by war; while the Government claimed no right to do more than to restrict the territorial enlargement of it. Neither party expected for the war, the magnitude, or the duration, which it has already attained. Neither anticipated that the *cause* of the conflict might cease with, or even before, the conflict itself should cease. Each looked for an easier triumph, and a result less fundamental and astounding.

Both read the same Bible, and pray to the same God; and each invokes His aid against the other. It may seem strange that any men should dare to ask a just God's assistance in wringing their bread from the sweat of other men's faces; but let us judge not that we be not judged. The prayers of both could not be answered; that of neither has been answered fully. The Almighty has His own purposes. "Woe unto the world because of offenses! for it must needs be that offenses come; but woe to that man by whom the offense cometh!" If we shall suppose that American slavery is one of those offenses which, in the providence of God, must needs come, but which, having continued through His appointed time, He now wills to remove, and that He gives to both North and South, this terrible war, as the woe due to those by whom the offense came, shall we discern therein any departure from those divine attributes which the believers in a living God always ascribe to Him? Fondly do we hope—fervently do we pray—that this mighty scourge of war may speedily pass away. Yet, if God wills that it continue, until all the wealth piled by the bond-man's two hundred and fifty years of unrequited toil shall be sunk, and until every drop of blood drawn with the lash, shall be paid by another drawn with the sword, as was said three thousand years ago, so still it must be said "the judgments of the Lord, are true and righteous altogether."

With malice toward none; with charity for all; with firmness in the right, as God gives us to see the right, let us strive on to finish the work we are in; to bind up the nation's wounds; to care for him who shall have borne the battle, and for his widow and his orphan—to do all which may achieve and cherish a just, and lasting peace, among ourselves, and with all nations.

Credits

Index